THE RONIN Y

The Ronin Years

Mas Oyama's Young Lion

BY

JUDD REID

with Anton Cavka and Norm Schriever

THE RONIN YEARS

Mas Oyama's Young Lion

Copyright ©2021 by Judd Reid. All rights reserved.

Artwork by Todd Reeves and Judd Reid.

DEDICATION

In honor and memory of my best friend, Anton Cavka.

This is for you, Tonnsa.

Six-foot peak!

This book is dedicated to my teacher, Master Sosai Oyama.

To my beautiful wife Mothana and my son Max, nothing can make a father prouder.

To my family, my rock, my mum, Kerry Rizzoli, Peter (Rizza), Alex, Georgia, and Marnie.

Howard Reid

Granny, Nan and Pop.

To the Cavka family: Marjorie, Anton Senior, Jacqui, Mike, and Nick.

To Norm Schriever, my brother. I am forever indebted to you and without you this book would not be possible.

Uchi Deshi brothers and Senpai's:

Nick Petttas, Yamakage San (Pink Panther), Karuda, Kato, Suzuki, Oshikiri, Ishida, Ligo, Shihan Sandor, Mohammad, Ishiguro Senpai, Yoneda Sempai, Hashimoto Senpai, Sugimura Senpai (The Razorback), Ishida Senpai (The Barber), and Yui Senpai (The Ranger).

Brunswick Dojo:

In loving memory of my first teacher, Ann Bradshaw. I miss you dearly Ann. RIP

Trevor Frith and Beckett.

Elwood Dojo:

My dear Shihan Eddie Emin, Joy Emin, Trevor E., and Billy Polly.

My mentor (older brother), Manny San.

Tiff K. and Tiff's gorgeous mum.

Nick Zav, Tommy M., Trifon, Garry Clarke, Mark the Hammer.

In loving memory of Anton Vojic.

My hero, Wada Sensei – I hope we can meet again one day soon.

The 100-man Fight Crew: Mac, JR, Tommy Z., Naoki, Hangover Ben, and Lewis.

Todd Reeves...thank you so much for all your magnificent artwork.

Emin

Kiley Baker

Tony W.

Nick Murphy

SHOP (Soldiers House Of Pain): Ned Vrselja, Michael Dugina, Costa Chondrus, Glen Williams, Dan Causovski, Chris Vlahogiannis, Anton Karaula, Aaron Goodson, Tristan Papadopoulos, Chris -Callum Brett,Tony - Lucas Karlusic, Warren Bentley.

Kym Osborne- wolfman

Noriyuki Tanaka Shihan RIP

Jack Roberts (nothing too hard to build!)

Steve Romic

Joe Haddad

Charlie Ridis

Stefan Seketa

David Caputto

Danny Madini

The Chevron: Paul, Vince and Mary

Mel Prest and Team Adrenalin family

Stephen Santo and family

Ronin Katz

DT Mohammad Bahrami-Mallooooo

Vivien, Hashba

Paul Phillips, Nick Beggs, Phil Jacobson, Steve, Kym, and Francesco.

Ben Robb RIP

Daniel Fox RIP

Nigel Marino RIP

Scott Powell - soldier!

Jason Griffiths - Blessed

Russ Sulaj - The Fridge

Lirim Sulaj

Patrick Pinto

Justin Ward

Goran Molin

George Kosinski

George Sallfedt

Daniel Casarella

Peter Velk - fighto!

Darren Jordan Shihan

Paul Cale Shibucho

Alicia, Rob, and Tiani Smith

Mark Ringwaltd

Dave - Crom

Ishi Sensei

Jim Phillips Shihan

Nathan Phillips

Callum Black

Todd Pantland, William, and Vincent

Tim Hook

Jet Tranter

Dean Booth - 100 more camps to go!

Travis, Cris, and Jordy

Michael Dent

Samuel Shields

Kristian Vergamalis

Kevin Brown - Irish warrior

Nick Kara

Nasar Kassab and family

Joe Sayah

Leo Dardha

Onrei Kompan

Terry, Alex Vorgiatzidis

Jason Sajadi, Ralph Burd, Saman Kadem

Micheal Abdulah

Matt - Tokyo Buddy

Sugihara Soshi, Mizuguchi Kancho, Ishikawa Shihan, Minami Shihan

Sifu McIness (The Colonel), Jr. McIness, Anong

The Kill Bills: Christina, Pim, Oliver, Minto, Isabella, Noi, Noot

Sakmongkol - superhuman

Mutt

Uchi Deshi's Thailand: Seb, Celine, Joe W., Vin, Rinny, Callum, Redfern family

International Seminars (beautiful hosts): Tom Callahan Shihan, Raul Dueno Sensei, Keith Hill Sensei, Christopher Frazier Sensei, Sebastien Mortreuil Sensei, Celine McClymont, Terry Birkett Shihan, Vinayak Shetty Sensei, Rinny Jr., Panos Vlachos Sensei, Mauricio Carranza, Mario Bolanos, Brain Fuller, Ernest Ong Sensei, Riki Young Sensei, Budiman Sutanto Sensei, Shihan Jerome Deti, Matthieu Morelle, Simeon Kyurchiev Sensei, Robert Wiklund Shihan, Sandor Brezovai Shihan, Darren Jordan Shihan, Alicia Smith Sensei, Rob Smith Sensei, Janelle Field Sensei, Frank Cirillo Sensei, Phil Cox Sensei, Peter Sensei, Dave Hughes Sensei, and the great Hanshi Shihan Eddie Emin, who started my whole journey in Kyokushin.

Chikara Dojo family:

Russ Sulaj's family, Ramo's family, David Udovic's family, Luke's family, Ellul family, Mandic family, Rees family, Giordano family, Usman's, Joe Strati family, Kassab family, Lachlan's family, Josh Cooke, Con Ogorman, Duncan Cameron, Mohammad Reazie, Bes brothers and all the Chikara students and families - you are the reason why I work so hard, as I'm always thinking of ways to make you stronger. It's been a real privilege and honor to train you.

Chikara young guns helping teach the junior classes Domenic, Genci, Maja, Alessandra, Daniel and Irini.

TABLE OF CONTENTS

Dedication	V
Foreword	Xiii
Chapter 1: School Of Hard Knocks	1
Chapter 2: Sweden	3
Chapter 3: The Great Sosai Mas Oyama	11
Chapter 4: Life On The Outside	19
Chapter 5: Gas Panic	27
Chapter 6: Politics	43
Chapter 7: The Ronin Years, 1996-2006	51
Chapter 8: Taking The Challenge Back To Japan	65
Chapter 9: Moving To Thailand To Step Up The Fight	73
Chapter 10: The Colonel	77
Chapter 11: The Wko Family	83
Chapter 12: Kancho Sugihara And The Rise Of The Wko	93

Chapter 13: Never Give Up	97
Chapter 14: Army Training And Swat	109
Chapter 15: The Gold Heist	117
Chapter 16: Training For The 2010 World Championship	125
Chapter 17: At Last	135
Chapter 18: Ufc Or The 100-Man Kumite	141
Chapter 19: King Of Tokyo	167
Chapter 20: Friday Night Tradition	175
Chapter 21: Training For The 100-Man Fight	185
Chapter 22: After The Fight	199
Chapter 23: Reflections	205
Chapter 24: The Brothers Reunite	211
Chapter 25: Return To Australia And The Documentary Release	215
Chapter 26: Family And Back Where I Belong	223
Chapter 27: The Mekong River	231
Chapter 28: Anton	237
Chapter 29: Less Than Zero	247
Chapter 30: A Whirlwind Tour	255
Chapter 31: Uchi Deshi Camp/Fighto	263
Chapter 32: Chikara	277
Afterword	285

FOREWORD

Meeting Anton Cavka was one of those chance encounters that completely change your life.

It was also the first time I heard the name Judd Reid, regaled with stories about a man who was almost a comic book superhero in magnitude. An Aussie immersed in the world of Japanese karate, Judd could do handstand pushups on his fingers, kick down trees, and once fought 100 men in a row.

Through him, I'd come to witness a mythical world of martial arts, circus-like feats of strength, and tales of Tokyo gangsters that were straight out of a movie. Judd Reid is a name I'd learn well - and a person I'd come to befriend and respect.

But that was much later.

First, there was Anton.

"You should meet this guy, Anton," the Facebook message from my good friend (or 'mate' in Australia) Clint read. Clint was from Melbourne, Australia, and someone I'd grown close to while traveling in Southeast Asia.

He knew I was staying in Phnom Penh, Cambodia for a few weeks, so he wanted to connect me with a guy named Anton who was there at that time, too. According to Clint, Anton was doing something or other with a karate documentary.

"Sure, just have him message me," I replied. An introductory message followed, and then a hello from Anton. He'd heard from Clint that I was a writer (or really just pretending to be one!) and wanted to enlist my help in promoting his new documentary film, *The 100-Man Fight*.

Anton suggested we meet up to chat about it. But the problem was that he was flying out of Cambodia that very morning.

"Maybe we can meet for a quick coffee if you're close," Anton messaged. It was optimistic thinking since you could spend hours stuck in traffic traversing the sprawling and chaotic city.

"Where are you staying?" He wrote.

"On a side street right near the riverside."

"Oh, me too. Which one?"

"I'm all the way down on 104 Street," I replied.

"What? I'm staying on 104, too. Which hotel?"

"The Pickled Parrot" I wrote.

"Me too!"

It turns out that out of hundreds of hotels in Phnom Penh, Anton and I were staying in the same one, only one floor apart. Conveniently, the Pickled Parrot also had a great 24-hour bar/

restaurant on the first floor. So, I shuffled downstairs at 6:30 am, just a few hours before his flight.

The Pickled Parrot was the perfect venue for our epic meeting. It was a relic from a bygone era when foreign journalists took shelter inside, drinking copiously as they spewed out typewritten pages about the Vietnam War and then the Cambodian Genocide under Pol Pot.

Almost half a century later, the infamous bar was still standing. Never closed for even one hour per year, it had a pool table, dart boards, plenty of rugby, cricket, and "footy" on the 1980s TV sets, a wooden bar shaped like a horseshoe, and a big fish tank in which it was a miracle anything still lived.

Even in the morning, a few grizzled old-timers mumbled into their beers, no one sure how many hours or decades they'd been sitting there. Several Khmer (Cambodian) youth wearing gold chains and sunglasses played pool, still drinking from the night before.

It was the kind of place where you wondered when – never if – the next knife fight would break out.

For guys like us, it was nirvana.

And there was Anton, sitting at a corner table in the windowless bar room, legs crossed like he was the CEO in a boardroom, not at a vagabond tavern in the most lawless nation in the world. To be honest, I don't even remember what Anton and I talked about the first hour.

He had that effect on people; you were caught up in his presence, his stern, ice-blue eyes seeing right through you. It was impossible not to be in the moment when you were with him, as he seemed to buzz with the possibility of what might happen next. And that energy was contagious, waking me up far more than the endless black coffee we slugged down.

Anton and I ordered huge Aussie brekkies and got into the meat of his new project. He told me about a man named Judd Reid, his best mate, who was a karate legend. Not only had Judd become a world champion, but he undertook something called the 100-man fight, a real-life Kumite where he fought and defeated 100 fighters in succession.

I was hooked.

Before he had to grab his bag, jump in a tuk tuk, and rush to the airport, Anton slipped me a DVD of the documentary. I went up to my room and watched it immediately, even more enthralled by the film's Herculean character, Judd Reid.

I wanted to help. Hell, I was just excited to be involved with those guys.

Soon after, I talked to Judd on the phone for about an hour, interviewing him for an article I'd write for the *Huffington Post*. I found him to be surprisingly soft-spoken and humble, like someone you're happy sits next to you on the first day of school, not one of the toughest men on the planet who doles out violence for a living. I did write that article for the *Huff Post*, called The Toughest Man Alive, just as Anton and Judd embarked on a worldwide barnstorming tour to promote the documentary.

Six months later, I finally got to meet Judd in Thailand where he lived. Instead of just meeting out at a restaurant, which was plenty convenient for me, he insisted on picking me up, always the gracious host. He wore a brand-new Boston Red Sox cap and filled the car ride with chirpy banter in his Aussie accent. I was sort of surprised that he was just a normal guy – I'd expected him to be 10 feet tall and practically levitate.

We talked a lot over dinner and a beer, and Judd invited me to his very first karate camp. I was to come as an observer, writing follow-up articles. I accepted and made travel preparations. Closer to the event, Judd invited me to join some of the camp's training if I wished, and said he'd have a gi ready for me.

At that point, Judd became Shihan Reid to me.

I wish I could tell you that I performed admirably in that first 12-day camp. In truth, I was out of shape, had never done karate before (just a little bit of boxing training), and ended up getting my ass kicked by every man, woman, and child in the camp.

But even after breaking three ribs and serving as the camp's resident punching bag, I fell in love with *Kyokushin* karate.

Since then, I've completed three of Shihan Reid's *uchi deshi* (live-in student) fight camps in Thailand. I'm still quite adept at blocking kicks with my face, but now I can almost give as good as I get.

But what *Kyokushin* karate has taught me is far more impactful than just techniques, wins or losses, or the color of my belt.

It's to fight, to never give up. It's that as long as you have breath. You keep moving forward. Because that's the only way to not only live,

But to truly be alive.

My training under Shihan Reid and my friendship with my brother Judd-O has taught me that within a literal fight is the fight for your life.

I've been through struggles for sure; as has Judd; as you have, too. But the struggle is the beauty. The journey IS the destination. And here we are, years later and a world away.

After that initial meeting, my friendship with Anton Cavka evolved, too. We worked on a few articles together, with late-night messaging flurries and rough drafts sent back and forth across the world. Soon, I had fooled Anton and Judd into thinking I was integral to the process, so they invited me back to Cambodia to work on the book together. I was thrilled to do it.

They got me a room at their hotel (a big upgrade from the Pickled Parrot), and I hopped on a flight from New York to Korea to Phnom Penh, Cambodia. I arrived on November 3, 2015, with very little sleep for almost two days. But I lit up when reunited with Anton and Judd. I remember standing there and realizing it was the first time I'd actually been in the same room with both of them.

We were looking forward to ten days of lifting weights and

hitting pads, splashing in the rooftop pool, exploring the streets of the bustling city, and, of course, writing, writing, and more writing.

It was going to be perfect, nirvana for guys like us.

Those were the plans, at least.

Six years later, it's still a privilege to know Judd Reid, both as Shihan and karate legend, and as a gracious and kind friend.

And that's why I'm so excited for people to read this book. In his first book, The Young Lions, we documented the legendary figure and his accomplishments in karate. But in The Ronin Years, we document the real man, Judd Reid; the emotions; the struggle; the inner fight; the journey – the LIFE.

And what a life it is.

I hope you enjoy reading The Ronin Years as much as I've enjoyed my small part in helping to write it. It's been an honor to know Judd Reid and Anton Cavka, and now truly an honor to bring you their story.

-Norm Schriever

Friend, student, and co-author

CHAPTER 1
SCHOOL OF HARD KNOCKS

A week after my graduation from the Young Lions program in 1993, I was still buzzing with excitement. I had successfully completed 1,000 days – three years – of the most intense training imaginable under the legendary founder of *Kyokushin* karate, Sosai Mas Oyama. Although I was the 68th student to successfully graduate from his *uchi deshi*, or live-in training program, which had been operating for 21 years, I was the very first foreigner to make it. But after all of that time, I sure didn't feel like a foreigner anymore and the *Honbu dojo* felt like home. I would stay in the dormitory until my 3rd *Dan* grading, and after that I had a plane ticket for Sweden – the other side of the world and a completely new experience after living in Japan for three years.

Lying there on my futon, I could hear *kiais* coming from the dojo. The orders from the teachers sounded far different when I wasn't in class, fighting it out and training with the rest of them. *Ichi Ni San, mawatte* (turn around), *Ichi Ni San …Kiai Kiai Kiaiaii!*

1

THE RONIN YEARS

The sounds of warriors in training echoed through the building, carrying their fighting spirit to every corner. Sosai Mas Oyama, my teacher, dedicated his life to creating a legacy of excellence at the *Honbu dojo*, a deeply spiritual place forged in strength and honor. It's a sensation I've only experienced a few times in my travels throughout life, including visiting the Acropolis in Athens.

The *Honbu dojo* was the epicenter of the world for all those who wanted to test themselves in *Kyokushin karate*. The School of Hard Knocks had produced some of the strongest men on the planet, before Sosai sent them overseas to spread *Kyokushin* and its philosophy.

It was my time to step up and honor that legacy. Sosai poured his precious time and energy – his whole life, really – into us, thousands of grueling hours of the most spartan training. And I sure wasn't going to let it go to waste.

In less than a week, I would be overseas and in a new country. I planned on representing Sosai and making him proud.

CHAPTER 2
SWEDEN

"Come ye trials and challenges; come life's big waves, for I am ready."

–Mas Oyama

About a week after graduation, there was always a big grading – usually for black belts first, second, third, fourth, and fifth *dans*. Sosai stood up and addressed all the students who were taking part in the grading. He encouraged everyone to dig deep and to do their very best. Sosai instructed them that the judges were looking at these points:

1. You have to be strong and possess both technique and speed.

2. Are you truly strong?

3. Are you fast enough?

4. Do you have the necessary skills?

5. Are your skills based on the correct concepts of *Kyokushin* karate?

Sosai also impressed upon the students the importance of engaging in what he called "elegant *Kumite*."

To do that, you should endeavor to evade all of your opponent's punches or kicks, while every one of your kicks or punches should be a threat.

Sosai said that to be the strongest is not an easy task. You must fight with all your might, but also pick your shots. Breathing – and in particular, exhalation of your breath – is very important. Especially in *tamashiwari* (the breaking of bricks, boards, baseball bats, etc.), it is your breathing that determines your success.

Defeating someone in a Kumite is the same. In a fight, it's crucial to fix your blow as your opponent breathes in. It's difficult to time that right, but if you can strike at the perfect opportunity, your opponent won't be able to breathe!

Kyokushin karate is the strongest karate, Sosai explained, because it's bare-knuckle karate and you don't use weapons. Work hard with a strong will, he always said. Based on his 50 years of experience, just pushing weights in the gym wouldn't make us strong.

Sosai went on to say that his hope was to see his students drop a bull with just a single strike. Sosai Oyama was famous for wrestling bulls with his bare hands!

"I am not a God; I am human," Sosai encouraged his students.

Sweden

"You and I eat the same things. So, the difference, I would humbly say, is the volume of training."

Sosai also said that we must return to nature, love the outdoors, and train outside. There, you can really push your limits. You cannot depend on machines, so training in nature should be exhausting and the techniques required are always demanding.

"The only secret is sweat!" Sosai said.

I was going for my third *dan* this time. Matsui Senpai was going for his fifth *dan* at the same time, and we were side by side, doing all the basics and *Kata*, literally doing the whole grading together over two days. The first day was technical with *Kihon* (basics), *Kata*, push-ups, sit-ups, squats, and kicking tennis balls that were hung by strings from the ceiling. Walking up and down the dojo floor on our palms, then fists, then fingers, was also part of the test. Three years of doing handstands every morning had turned our fists into weapons and all uchi deshi's were expected to be able to do handstands on their fists and fingers.

The second day was all fighting. For my third *Dan*, I had to do a 30-man *Kumite*. Nick Pettas, Walter (Wally) Schnaubelt, and Kou Tanigawa were all going for their gradings too, so we had to fight each other as well as all the *uchi deshi*. You wouldn't believe it, but the Ranger (Yui Senpai) who only months before had demanded that Nick and I pack up and leave, was the official judge for my 30-man *Kumite*.

In those days, getting your first *dan* required ten fights, second *Dan* required 20, and third *Dan* required 30. But these fights were full-on, almost at tournament level, not like they are today. You would get smashed and there was a referee scoring the fights like in a tournament. As luck would have it, my ref was Yui *Senpai*. But you know what? He encouraged me and cheered me on! It was incredible how his attitude toward me had changed in just six months.

When the Ranger told Nick and I to pack our bags and leave six months earlier, it fueled my soul with fire and determination to train harder. I thank him for this now and all is forgiven.

Honbu was a school of gladiators, plain and simple. There was no room for being soft. You had to suck it up and persevere with whatever crazy orders you were given, no matter what was going on at the time. Thank god it wasn›t any other way. I've craved that environment since I was a young kid, and I sure as hell got it.

I successfully passed my *san dan* grading. A week later, in late March 1993, just like Wada Sensei before me, I went overseas to Sweden to teach. I remember the first week arriving in Sweden at Ostersund, a small town of about 50,000 people in the north. It was covered in snow with freezing temperatures outside and there was not much at all to do except sit inside and try to stay warm. It was a huge shock coming from high-rise Tokyo to mostly two-story houses. At that time of year, it wasn't getting light until about 11 a.m. and got dark again around 3 p.m.!

I remember one night I was lying in bed in my basement bedroom at the house I was staying at. It was a nice house and a decent room, but I was totally alone in the dark. For three years,

I'd gotten used to my *uchi deshi* brothers right beside me in the dorm. As a second-year student, I was a teacher in the *Honbu*. I won a major regional tournament in my third year and had passed my third *dan* grading. I should have been on top of the world.

But here I was in this basement room instead, in a small town that was freezing cold outside. It felt like solitary confinement. I was incredibly lonely thinking, "What have I done?"

That night, I rolled over to one side in a ball and cried myself to sleep. I felt I had made a big mistake.

My first month in Ostersund in the perpetual dark, cold, and snow, I was very depressed. I had really needed to get out of Japan and have a holiday from Tokyo and the big city and rules and regulations. But I completely regretted going to Sweden the first two weeks because I was just sitting around inside during the day and then teaching in the dark at night. However, I soon adjusted to the routine and environment and things began to improve.

Next, I went to Stockholm for a few weeks to Dolph Lundgren's dojo under Brian Fitkin Shihan. I remember being really happy to leave Ostersund. Not only was Stockholm warmer, but I also gave a good display of full-contact sparring and a baseball bat breaking demonstration in front of the legendary actor who played Ivan Drago! Gorin Molin, a student of Fitkin Shihan, organized for me to teach at the Stockholm dojo. We became good friends and training partners. He fought in the European championships and came in third, which was a sensational accomplishment.

Then, it was onto Gothenburg for another few weeks, teaching at Howard Collins' Shihan's dojo. Collins' Shihan is from Wales and Fitkin Shihan is from England. Both of them had moved to Sweden in the late '70s and are legends in the *Kyokushin* world, so it was a privilege to teach at their *dojos*.

After about three months, I was moved again, this time to Orebro, a beautiful university town in south central Sweden. All of the places I stayed in Sweden were beautiful, but by the time I reached Orebro, it was the beginning of July, so the weather had warmed up and I got a sense of just how beautiful the country could be. I taught karate in the day and worked part time doing security at a local bar, enjoying a bit of fun with the local girls who were all tall, blonde, and beautiful. I had a golden time.

George Sallfedt and Bo Johansson had organized for me to teach at their dojo. It was a great pleasure teaching in this pretty town, and I was really enjoying my life.

The club where I worked was called Stronpus, and there was a lot of trouble between the local kids and a group of kids who were refugees from Iraq. At one point, there was a big fight between five Iraqi kids and security. They were out and out troublemakers, darting around and fighting other patrons, so we kicked them all out. They mouthed off and said they'd be back.

Later that night, two of the Iraqis waited for one of our guys named Gregor Kosinski to come home to his apartment. He was training with me at the time, and he beat those two kids up and then called the police. Outside of this one incident, it was a peaceful, happy time, and I left Sweden with very positive memories of the place.

After my Swedish tour of duty, I returned to Japan in October to train in the *Honbu*, this time living outside the school and fending for myself. I think Sosai wanted me to stay on as a teacher, but I just didn't realize it at the time. The usual procedure was that *uchi deshi* would graduate and leave the dormitory, teaching elsewhere for six months to a year, and then return to Japan to open up their own school, eventually becoming branch chiefs. But I was the first foreigner to ever graduate from the *uchi deshi* program, so things were always going to be different for me. This was uncharted territory.

What was I supposed to do next? Try to buck all social norms in Japan and open a dojo as a foreigner there? Head home to Australia and open one there? To say I was lost at this time would be a huge understatement.

I moved into a tiny apartment, barely the size of a bathroom, and was trying to decide what the next step in my life would be. The next World Tournament was to be held in 1995, but my mind wasn't on that just yet. I was at a crossroads and had no idea where I was supposed to go and what I was supposed to do next.

CHAPTER 3:
THE GREAT SOSAI MAS OYAMA

"The best reason for learning karate is to develop character- to make a good man first and a strong man second. This must be understood to advance."

--Mas Oyama

Late in December, I returned back to Australia for the first time in three and a half years. Initially I thought I'd just stay for Christmas, but I ended up staying almost four months. I'd made some money teaching in Sweden and thought about perhaps returning to Australia to teach, but I immediately didn't like it.

So, I returned to Japan in February, and although I was no longer living in the *Honbu* as an *uchi deshi*, I found a cheap apartment in nearby Ekoda so I could go to the *Honbu* to train three to four days a week.

One day in April of 1994, I came back from shopping and saw

a note on my apartment door. I opened it up and read it. It said, "I'm very sorry, Judd, to inform you that Sosai Oyama has passed away. My deepest condolences." It was written by Big Dave, the American.

I kept reading over and over, not believing what I was seeing. This couldn't be! I just stared at the note, standing there motionless inside my apartment. My whole body crumbled, and I broke down crying. I remember putting my head face-down into the pillow because I was crying so loudly, I couldn't control my emotions.

After composing myself, I called *Honbu,* and one of the uchi deshi answered the phone, confirming Sosai had passed away. I jumped on a train and headed straight to Ikebukuro. When I arrived, there were hundreds of people there. *"This was a nightmare,"* I thought. Surely this couldn't be happening. People were crying, and they had their heads bowed low, making soft conversation.

That night, I laid in bed and wept until I fell asleep. I was alone, in a tiny room, some foreign kid who had trained under the great Oyama, now lying curled up in a ball, powerless. I kept thinking; *my poor master is dead. This is inconceivable. I might as well be dead too. He was still so strong when I last saw him. Did he know he was sick?*

To this day, it's still a mystery how Sosai died. Some say it was throat cancer or lung cancer, although he never smoked. There are even conspiracy theories about how it really happened. If he knew that he was sick, Sosai hid it very well. One thing is for sure: There will never be another Mas Oyama.

He died on April 26 and his funeral was held six days later. People came from all over the world to attend. From Shigeru Oyama to Howard Collins and Bobby Lowe, just about everyone involved in *Kyokushin* for the past 30 years came to the funeral – thousands of people. People who I had seen in magazines but never met were even there. It was like a who's who of *Kyokushin* karate history. I remember Matsui standing side-by-side next to Kuristina, Mas Oyama's daughter, and Kuristina's mum. The closed coffin was at the front of the shrine, and we all walked past and bowed. The branch chiefs formed the guard of honor at the end, and everyone paid their respects to Mas Oyama then walked through the formation of guards on the way out. The shrine was in Tokyo, but Sosai was eventually buried at Mitsumine Shrine in Chichibu in Saitama where the winter camps were held. It was fitting that he was laid to rest in those same mountains where he'd trained for three years by himself.

Sosai's death came as a huge shock to me. I heard that before his death, he was in his *dogi,* his karate uniform, continuously for three days. I remember speaking to Nick about how Sosai passed away, but even Nick himself didn't know what was true. He'd graduated just a few weeks earlier, one of the last of Sosai's Young Lions. Although Nick had heard rumors that Sosai wasn't well, he had no idea that things were this bad. We were both in absolute despair, sick with disbelief, and crippled like our own father had just died.

This incredible man had inspired millions of people around the world. His superhuman strength was like no other, but his best quality as a human being was his compassion and beautiful nature. Here are a few examples of Sosai's character. This interview was done in the early '90s in America for *Black Belt Magazine*.

Cameron Quinn is the interpreter for Sosai. They were very close, and Cameron did a magnificent job translating, really showcasing what a remarkable man Sosai was.

Q: What is *Kyokushin* to you?

A: Just like karate *Kyokushin* is my life.

Q: What do you see for the future of *Kyokushin*?

A: I'm not a God so I can't really see the future of America or the world in fact, so I can't really see the future of what is going to happen to *Kyokushin* in Japan. But I'm quite certain that *Kyokushin* will continue to expand and grow fruitfully throughout the world. The seed of *Kyokushin* has been placed in every country around the world.

Q: How many people have studied this style?

A: I can't even tell you myself, there have been so many, but registered we have over 10 million.

Q: *Kyokushin* is considered a hard style, maybe the hardest style in the world, what kind of people can we expect to come out of the style?

A: The most important thing that we develop is their attitude and spirit. Of course, they train a hard style, they become strong, but the most important thing is that strength is pointless without a pure attitude. If I could describe the true spirit of *Kyokushin* it is simply this: the person should have their head bowed in humility while the eyes are kept high in hope, reserved in speech but they have a very broad heart, always thinking of others, at the basis of all their attitude is a true love for their parents and a constant desire to be of service to other people. That is the true *Kyokushin* spirit.

I learned that Mas Oyama also received a constant flow of mail from students and fans throughout Japan. As he became a legend, these correspondences grew more frequent, almost daily. Many asked about his students who had left the dojo or been expelled. For whatever reason, people were interested in them. Anyway, Sosai replied to those particular letters with great anguish. I wanted to share one such fan's letter to Oyama Sosai, along with his reply.

A letter to Sosai Oyama:

Dear Masutatsu Oyama,

I have never met you in person, but as a great fan of *Kyokushin*,

THE RONIN YEARS

I have read all of your books. In the past, many students have left you to start their own school. It is truly disappointing. They're living off the full contact karate you created. As a pioneer, you must have endured hardship in the past when your karate was considered heretical. What happened to the spirit? *Kyokushin* honors the spirit of harmony. It's a family. But I have become doubtful. I feel sorry for you. That's why I decided to write to you. Oyama Sensei, as a Japanese you are the pride of the world.

Sosai Oyama's reply:

Dear Sir,

Thank you for your letter. As you said, we have not met. But I appreciate you knowing me and thus writing to me. As far as the students who have decided to leave me, I have only myself to blame.

I feel I was born to be a budo-ka, not a leader. *Kyokushin* karate has grown into a huge entity with 400,000 students in Japan and 10 million worldwide. I wanted to live like Musashi Miyamoto, but I am now the head of an organization, and managing it is very difficult.

I am almost 70, but it is only now that I realize how difficult human relationships are. I have come to feel the vanities and sorrows of humans.

Thank you for your kind thoughtfulness. Right now, I have many students I can trust close to me. I am also aware that we have many loyal supporters like you. Thank you for your advice, and your kind and honorable view of *Kyokushin*.

I sincerely hope you continue to support *Kyokushin* warmly as always.

Kyokushin kaikan,

Masutatsu Oyama.

Sosai was a father figure to both Nick and me, a father figure to many who were fortunate enough to spend time with him. He will never be forgotten, and I will try my very best to carry on his legacy and do him proud.

CHAPTER 4
LIFE ON THE OUTSIDE

浪人

"No matter how strong the rival, they just will always win."

–Mas Oyama

I returned to Australia in May of 1994, lost and distressed after Sosai's passing. It was good to be back with my family and old friends, and I soon cheered up and stayed a few months, remaking old acquaintances and taking a break. Just as I was graduating as a Young Lion, most of my old friends were finishing their university degrees in the middle of the biggest recession Australia had seen in decades. On TV, there were scenes of hundreds of people lining up to apply for a job at the Sizzler steak house – many with engineering, science, and economics degrees in hand.

So, many of my friends decided to travel for a year, which they call a "gap year" these days, with the hope that the job situation would improve by the time they came back. A few of us – Nick Murphy, Anton Cavka, his brother, Mike, and me – had a game of golf at Essendon Golf Course, my old stomping grounds. They were a good bunch of guys and by the end of that round of golf, I had talked them all into coming to Japan.

It wasn't my initial intention, but it also wasn't a very hard sell! They were all planning to go to Europe anyway – the standard trail was to go to the Greek islands, then the running of the bulls in Spain, and on to Italy, France, and then Oktoberfest in Germany. In those days, all the flights from Australia to Europe stopped in Asia anyway. Just as importantly, there was easy money to be made in Japan by teaching English or other odd jobs for foreigners.

If teaching English wasn't your thing, you could make a good living in Japan and save money for traveling being a caddie or ski instructor. Foreigners were still a rarity in Japan in those days, and $50 an hour to teach English was great money for a poor, out-of-work graduate trying to save for Europe.

In October 1994, Anton, Joe Sayah, and I flew to Tokyo and moved into what was called a *gaijin* house in Nakano. *Gaijin* is the Japanese word for foreigner, literally meaning "outside person." As all houses in Japan need a guarantor, even for the Japanese, innovative foreigners would set up houses, get Japanese guarantors, and then rent them to other foreigners for a hefty profit. It was a good business in the days before Airbnb.

Those were interesting times. Anton, Joe, and I used to walk the streets and locals would stare and point at us on the way to and from the restaurants and gym. We did a lot of weight training at a place called Unicorn Gym near the old *Honbu* in Ikebukuro, and often ate at one of two restaurants – the Texas Steak House or Ootoya, which served traditional Japanese food, but we called the "chicken restaurant" because we usually ordered the chicken cuts with rice. These were a new breed of discount restaurants that had only just begun to spring up. Meals were about $10, and the turnover was high. Compared to the average price of $50 for lunch in those days, it was a real revolution in dining – and, really, the only places we could afford to eat out.

I'd met Joe through Nick Zav when I first got back to Australia earlier in the year, and we immediately hit it off. He was the main instructor at William Chung's kung fu *dojo* in Melbourne, and at 23, one of the youngest *Sifus* in history. His nickname was Dragon Joe, and he was lightning quick with his hands, a great fighter and someone who, if he was your friend, would guard you like some sort of protective force field. He would gently push you to the side of the road if a truck or car came past in the small streets and stand between you and it as if to somehow shield you from any danger. Sifu Joe Sayah was a very good man, and Tokyo would soon embrace him as a local hero.

We had been in Japan for about one month when the three of us realized we needed to find work quickly. Tokyo is still an extremely expensive city, but probably the most expensive city in the world at the time. The first thing we did was search in the Tokyo classifieds for English teacher jobs. It was the most popular job for westerners living in Tokyo, so we found a few possibilities. The next morning, Joe and I suited up and went in for an interview in a downtown office building.

I never saw myself as an English teacher, but I needed work desperately if I wanted to continue living in Japan. The interviews with the company, Nova, went pretty smoothly, and I think I answered all the questions correctly. Everything was going well, and I was feeling optimistic - until our elevator ride down to the ground floor.

The Nova employees who had interviewed us were nice enough to escort us down to the ground floor. But in the elevator, Joe started talking to me about training and got all pumped up. He started striking the elevator with an open-hand strike, much to the consternation of our potential new bosses, who had no idea what he was talking about. Joe struck the door so hard once that the whole elevator shook, momentarily coming to a halt before restarting again immediately.

Joe apologized for striking the door but kept on talking about training like nothing had happened. By the time the doors opened at the ground floor, I couldn't help but notice that the Nova staff were wide-eyed in confusion and more than a little scared.

Sure enough, I called them up the next day to see if we got the jobs, but they said sorry, but we both didn't meet the requirements. Thinking about it now, that was never going to happen after one of their crazy new perspective employees started fighting the elevator!

We were increasingly desperate. Luckily, I bumped into one of my Japanese friends a few days later, Ichiro, whom I had known for about a year. I'm not exactly sure what he was doing for work at the time, but he had close ties to the *Yakuza*, or Japanese mafia. Ichiro suggested that we all catch up for dinner that night. Since Anton had a bunch of interviews lined up for the next day, Joe and I went to meet him.

Now, this is when the story gets really strange.

The restaurant where we were meeting at was a fancy Italian place in Harajuku, a lively and modern place, where multimillion-dollar clothing stores displayed the latest fashions and Tokyo trend setters packed the hottest new restaurants. We were arriving on the sidewalk when Joe and I were suddenly struck on the top of our heads by falling wood planks.

Smash!

What the hell just happened?

The impact could have been much worse, and we were more confused than anything. I quickly looked behind me, and about six more wood planks came crashing to the ground simultaneously.

Joe and I were so puzzled that we were at a loss for words. Where the hell did this wood come from?

There were no buildings close enough for the wood to have accidentally fallen off, or even been tossed off the top of a roof. There were no cars passing by near us so it's not like someone had thrown the wood at us as they sped by.

And the planks had fallen on us with some serious force, like they'd dropped a long way. How we weren't seriously injured or sent to the hospital, I still don't understand. But Joe and I were completely spooked. What was extra strange was that the six-foot planks looked really old, like from a dilapidated apartment building or something. But all the buildings around us were new and modern.

I'm not one to get superstitious, but this really had us baffled and scared.

By the time we reached the restaurant a few minutes later, we didn't say much to each other, but we both had the feeling as though maybe we shouldn't be there.

Entering the Italian restaurant, we saw Ichiro seated at the back corner with a few of his mates. We walked over casually and sat down.

My mate, Ichiro, who I hadn't seen since before going to Sweden a year earlier, was friendly as always, but his acquaintances weren't. They stood out like sore thumbs: matching dark suits, Elvis Presley-style pompadours combed back, Louis Vuitton man-purses, and fat, gold Rolex watches. That was all standard Yakuza style for the '90s and it was obvious to me that my friend had gotten heavily involved with the notorious Japanese underworld.

Ichiro didn't beat around the bush, asking directly if Joe I would be keen to work with him. He explained that he had an office in Nishi Azabu which is an upper-class suburb in Tokyo and had about 20 guys running casinos for him. Casinos are illegal in Japan, so they're almost exclusively run by the Yakuza and kept very discreet. Ichiro wanted us to be debt collectors and security.

Now you must remember that Joe and I were still shaken up from getting hit on the head by falling wood planks from the sky, and now we had an open door to the Japanese mafia if we chose to walk through it. But we both saw what happened outside as a bad omen or a sign that we shouldn't get involved. I told my mate that we had to go, politely thanked him for dinner, and we left the restaurant, looking towards the sky the entire walk home.

Returning safely back to our apartment in Nagano, we caught up with Anton and told him the story.

He thought we were nuts and then admitted it was a really strange happening. I had encouraged both Anton and Joe to come to Japan, so I felt a responsibility to take care of them and to make sure everything was going to be OK. We were young and had each other's backs, but there was no doubt Tokyo was a dragon that wasn't to be tempted or trifled with.

Anton had a bunch of English teaching jobs lined up. He was the clever one so he could pick and choose which employment he was going to get. So, Joe and I decided to make our way to Roppongi in search of doing security in one of the night clubs there.

CHAPTER 5: GAS PANIC

浪人

I remember that one of the first bars we went to was called Gas Panic, managed by a guy named Toki – a bilingual and streetwise Tokyo local. Gas Panic was on the third floor of a nondescript building, down a side street off the main Roppongi Dori Street. You took a small elevator to get up to it, and as soon as the elevator doors opened, you were met with the deafening roar of pumped-up American music – lots of *Metallica* and *Rage Against the Machine*. The place was always packed, and there were signs on the wall everywhere saying, "You must be drinking to stay inside Gas Panic."

Burly foreign waiters in Gas Panic t-shirts would walk around telling customers to order a fresh drink if they weren't already holding one. If they refused to buy another round, they would get physically thrown out by security! With a dynamic like this, the bar half-full of Marines and the crowd fueled by non-stop alcohol, you can only imagine how many fights would break out each night.

Joe and I asked Toki if he needed security, but he said that they were fine for the moment. We stayed around and watched for a while. At one point he pulled Joe aside and said, "Joe, you look like a tough guy and I'd probably hire you for some work, but your mate looks like a bit of a pretty boy." I didn't hear that over the music, but Joe told me on the train on the way home. I had to laugh at that one!

We got home that night to meet Anton and tell him how everything went. Anton suggested I take in some videos from my tournament fights, but I decided that wasn't necessary. The three of us all slept in the one six-mat tatami room upstairs, so it was almost like being back in the dojo. At $1,000 a month, it was all we could afford. We slept almost side by side when our futons were rolled out, but luckily for us, we were all such great mates that we got along well. The remainder of the house was populated with Nick, a young rich Aussie kid whose parents were doctors, Collin, a gay Canadian guy in the two other rooms upstairs, and an Aussie couple from Perth, John and Kathy, downstairs. Well, maybe it wasn't quite like the dorm, but we all got on well and living in a residential Japanese suburb was a daily adventure.

The next night, Joe and I decided to return to Gas Panic and re-plead our case for work. We arrived just in time to find the place surrounded by police cars and ambulances, with Toki being carried out on a stretcher, his head all bandaged up. Apparently, the security guards had kicked out a couple of Africans, and they came back with 40 of their friends and beat up everyone in the bar – including the security, the manager, and even all the bar staff.

Gas Panic

Toki, from his stretcher, recognized us and said, "If you still want the job, you can start tomorrow night." So that was the beginning of our crazy year fighting bad guys in Roppongi.

It's hard to believe that in such a peaceful country like Japan, a place like Roppongi exists. The old nickname for the area was High Touch Town, announced in large signage on the highway that passed overhead. But there is nothing "high touch" about Roppongi. It was like the Wild West in those days. The bar clientele were about 70% to 30% Japanese to foreigners. The white foreigners were Marines, English teachers, or bankers mostly, but the bankers didn't come to Gas Panic. Then there was a mix of Nigerians, Iranians, and Japanese Brazilians that made up the rest of the bar crowd.

Parts of our everyday life in Japan were like something out of a movie. Anton and I were just walking home one day and when we turned the corner onto our street, we saw about 20 Japanese Brazilians carrying chains, baseball bats, and other assorted weapons, all dressed in bandanas, black t-shirts, and ripped jeans. We spun around to see another gang coming from the other direction – with the same sort of numbers, but pure Japanese.

Not knowing exactly what to do next, we stood back to see how this was going to pan out. Just in the nick of time, about 30 Japanese police in full riot gear came tearing down the street, and both gangs scattered into the night. These were not normal times.

In fact, there were a lot of earthquakes around that period – every day, in fact. People were constantly talking about the "big one" coming next. On January 17, 1995, it finally hit. It was the Great Hanshin Earthquake, measuring 7.2 on the Richter scale, and the epicenter was about 20 km from Kobe. It leveled the city and killed thousands of people, a real wake-up call for the Japanese. They thought they were prepared for a big earthquake, but this proved just how wrong they were.

Buildings came crashing down and fires started everywhere. All the highways into Kobe buckled so emergency services had no way to get in or out. It took the rest of Japan about three days just to reach the survivors, and two weeks to provide basic services. Most people literally just walked out of the most devastated areas and moved into tent cities on the outskirts or moved in with relatives in other cities.

Working the door at Gas Panic, Joe and I were experiencing our own seismic activity. It seemed like every bad guy in Tokyo came down to try his luck fighting us security guards. Joe, as I said, was an incredible street fighter with blindingly quick hands, and he was always ready for trouble. Big guys of all nationalities would come down and fight other patrons and then us when we attempted to kick them out. Joe wasn't one to be trifled with, however, and he would give everyone one chance and one chance only.

If you were fighting or threatening to fight and you heard the words "put your hands down" from Joe, you either complied or you paid the consequences. Kung fu fighters have a very different style of punching from karate fighters, and often use the back of their fists in a forward moving circular motion. Joe could deliver six or seven punches to the head before the offending patron hit the ground. These were bad seeds: thugs, bullies, and gangsters of all sorts. But Joe didn't care who they were. He beat up nearly every bad guy in Roppongi and, in the process, the strangest thing happened.

These bad guys, realizing they couldn't beat Joe, often came back and apologized and became part of what I called Joe's Army, helping out when the numbers were against us. It was a crazy time, and Joe became a huge celebrity in Roppongi. You literally couldn't walk ten meters down the main street with him without people yelling his name and running over to greet him. Crowds of people would surround him wherever he went like he was a movie star. He even fought in one of the original K1 tournaments.

One night, early on in our new jobs, Anton and double doctor Nick came out to our bar after drinking a couple of bottles of hard liquor that Anton brought over duty free on the plane. They were clearly drunk but in good spirits, and after a while asked us where else they should go. I suggested a bar a couple of streets down on the left, with a red door they couldn't miss.

About an hour later, Anton came back to Gas Panic covered in blood. Joe and I were shocked at the state he was in. He had a broken nose, smashed lips, cuts all over his scalp, and his face was swollen up like the Elephant Man. He told us that he and Nick were dancing on the tables in the red door bar when Nick fell off, and the Marine bouncers dragged him outside and started kicking him on the street. Anton stepped in and tried to defend him, punching the biggest guy smack in the head. But another six Marines ran out of the bar, joining the four already there, and they really went to town on him. He tried to cover his head as they kicked into him, but he was backed up against a wall, and his head began smashing against it with every kick until he fell unconscious.

Anton was in a terrible way, and Joe and I immediately said, "We've got to get you to a hospital, mate. Let's call an ambulance." He insisted, however, that he felt no pain. The liquor he had consumed previously had fixed all that. And now was not the time for medical treatment - now was the time for payback! I even remember him looking at our disbelieving faces and saying, "Listen, guys, don't look at all the blood. To me, it may as well be water. I can't feel any pain. Now let's go get these guys."

So, Joe said, "Let's go!" and off the three of us went. The next bar was a couple of blocks down, and Anton was racing ahead of us like he was in some sort of mad rush to get back there and even the score.

He turned the corner where the bar was, with us just behind him, and this tall American at the front door said, "Oh, you again. Back for more, are you?" With that, Anton threw an almighty right cross that caught him square on the chin. Like a scene out of a movie, the 6'3" Marine went flying through the air and landed in a pile of garbage bags next to the front door. Anton was never a trained fighter, but he was strong and never backed down from a fight if challenged.

Joe, beside me, yelled out an almighty, *"Ishhhhaaa!"* when Anton floored this guy, and like angry ants, all the other Marines started flooding out of the bar and attacking us. They were all big guys who'd spent a lot of time in the gym, but they were no match for Joe and me. One by one they dropped. Punches, thigh kicks, elbows, whatever it took, we needed to take them down fast before their sheer size and numbers overwhelmed us. Joe reveled in avenging our best friend. I just thought of it as being in a tournament with multiple opponents at once!

In the end, they were all out cold or lying on the ground, unable or unwilling to get back up. The tall guy, who was apparently the head of security, got up out of the rubbish on one knee and pleaded with Joe, "Enough, please, no more."

Joe looked deep into his eyes, pointed over in Anton's direction and said, "You see my friend?" and gave him one last knockout blow to the head. We were hearing police sirens by now, so I put Anton in a taxi and told the taxi driver where to take him. When the driver turned around and saw Anton, he almost had a heart attack, but I assured him in Japanese that Anton would be okay if he took him to the address that I gave him.

We woke up the next day to find Anton and Nick both looking like they had been hit in the face by a truck. They were in bad shape, and they both spent about a month watching videos and sucking on aspirins to dull the pain. Everything was so expensive in Japan that they both decided they could fix themselves. Anton said this wasn't the first time he'd copped a hiding from a gang of thugs, and he even re-broke his own nose to put it back in place.

Eventually, when he healed up, Anton took an English teaching job about an hour south of our Nakano house, and Joe and I continued working in Gas Panic. That fight just enhanced our reputation even further.

Now, I don't condone street fighting or wanton violence, but in my eyes, this year I spent in the Roppongi war zone was out of this world. We never started a fight, were always polite to regular customers, and never beat anyone up who hadn't tried to attack our staff or us first. They were almost always bigger in size and numbers than us, and the fights were fair. We were fighting the bullies, standing up for ourselves, and making the bad guys pay. Just as Sosai said so many times to us *uchi deshi*: "*Nande karate yaru no?* – Why are you doing karate?" And his answer: "*Kenka no tame ni tsuyoke nare kara* – So you can be strong and defend yourself in a street fight."

Scott Powell also worked the door with Joe and I at Gas Panic. He was a U.S. Marine stationed at the Yokosuka base just outside of Tokyo who joined when he was just 20 years old and fought in the Gulf War in Iraq in the '90s.

We didn't talk about it much, but for sure being a U.S. Marine in the Middle East would have been full-on. He definitely looked the part, standing over six-foot-tall with a bodybuilder's physique and covered in tattoos, his chipped-tooth grin the only warning that he was always ready to throw punches first and ask

Gas Panic

questions later.

Scott wasn't supposed to take on security work or any other work while in the Marines, but he used to hang out with us at the front door on the weekends and we all became good mates.

He would even stay over at our place and literally sleep in the doorway of our small apartment for lack of a better sleeping area! After all, as a Marine, he really didn't care – and probably had slept in worse conditions.

Finally, Toki, the manager of Gas Panic, offered him a job. Despite the fact that he didn't have the blessing of the U.S. government, he took the job. Not only was it an extra bit of cash for him, but he was already part of our team and always had our back.

Far from being a trained karate fighter or a Kung fu master like Joe, Scott's pugilistic discipline was straight street brawling. He was fearless, hit first, hit hard, and put all of his muscle-bound frame behind it.

I've literally seen Scott (and Joe) in dozens of fights and can't really think of any time when someone clearly got the best of him. It didn't matter how outnumbered or outgunned he was, Scott would never back down or leave a friend.

Just one example comes to mind, and I wasn't even there that night. I heard the next day of an incident where Scott and Joe punched on with some foreigners who were in Japan for a Judo tournament. They were all from Belgium and wearing their team jackets.

These foreigners were getting soused (which is certainly no crime in a club) but started getting aggressive, shoving a few patrons and generally exhibiting bad behavior.

Scott and Joe asked them to leave and escorted them downstairs towards the front door. But as they walked out, one of the guys pushed Scott hard, sending him flying into the wall.

Big mistake.

Scott and Joe instantly retaliated with all their fury, sending the drunken judo fighters reeling. They held no punches back, and at the end, the whole Judo crew was laid out on the ground.

Scott and Joe were just defending themselves fairly - after all, they were outnumbered, and these foreigners started the fight with an unprovoked attack.

The Japanese are so polite and respectful, but sometimes, foreigners are a different story, coming to the club to be disrespectful and cause trouble. Well, they came to the wrong club that night, as Scott and Joe weren't about to let anyone get away with it.

One night while we were all working the door, the Tokyo police suddenly turned up in full riot gear. They carried shields with their metal batons drawn, and face guards pulled down ready for battle.

The site of a Japanese SWAT team was definitely a shock. What the hell was going on?!

I quickly asked in Japanese if everything was OK and what

was happening. Scott and Joe couldn't speak Japanese, and I wanted to defuse the situation quickly and try to work out what they wanted.

"We have come for him," one policeman answered in Japanese, pointing towards Joe.

There were four of them, and I had never seen police dressed like that before. Well, only in the movies. Something must have really triggered them to come ready to go to war like this.

"What is the problem?" I asked, remaining polite.

"We need Joe to come with us to make a statement," one of the policemen answered.

"What happened? What was it?" I asked again.

By now, the whole club had become silent, and the attention was on us.

"We just need him to come to the police station," he demanded, but wouldn't answer any more questions.

Joe, Scott, and I weren't really worried anymore, just puzzled. There had been an incident the night before with some Japanese men - which was very rare, so maybe it had something to do with that?

The Japanese police are straight and respectable, not corrupt or malicious in any way. They do everything by the book, so I wasn't really nervous about violence breaking out, just very curious.

The foreigners in that area of Roppongi ran amuck, so I'm

sure the police didn't know how to handle us sometimes, and they might go overboard in their methods.

A few more words were exchanged between us, until Joe smiled at them and said, "I'll go with you guys - no worries."

Joe›s smile and his nature would win anyone over.

«We will drop him back after being interviewed,» the policeman answered in a now-friendly tone.

Joe left with the police and returned after only two hours later, grinning and telling us the story. To be honest with you, I can't even recall why they took Joe away, and Joe doesn't even remember the reason to this day, either. But we both definitely have a clear memory of these police walking into the Gas Panic that night.

Joe was such a lovable character, he won them all over and was even arm wrestling them all by the end of the interview, and pretty much made good mates with them all. We never heard from the police again after this incident!

But it wasn't just boozers, brawlers, and Japanese partiers who showed up at our club – we had notable names from the fight world, too. In the 1990s, K1 (kickboxing) was huge, as well as Pancrese (an MMA-like show). After their events in Tokyo, some of the fighters would rock out in our club.

Peter Aerts, Jerome La Banner, Mike Bernardo, Bas Rutten, and Ken Shamrock were some of the big names that came in to have drinks and say hi.

Gas Panic

I found that they were all super friendly guys, and of course, there never was trouble. I specifically remember Peter Artz hanging out with us at the front door. He was such a friendly guy and a huge superstar in Japan. The best fighters are usually humble, respectful, and just want to chill. I think they enjoyed hanging out at our club because they were left relatively alone and could relax and party without getting mobbed by fans.

However, once they hit the street, people would rush in from everywhere, asking for signatures, taking photos, and even trying to touch them. They were gods in Japan, there's no doubt about it. The K1 days was a golden era in kickboxing for sure. Australia's own Sam Greco was a part of this golden era, and a legend in the sport. Later came Peter Graham, John Hallford and, of course, the biggest superstar of them all - Andy Hug. They all started with *Kyokushin* karate, by the way.

Many people in *Kyokushin* thought that I was some kind of hard-drinking playboy in Roppongi in 1995, but I just avoided the *Honbu* due to all of the politics going on. I never drank in those days at all, and I was still training, just not at the *Honbu*. In my head, I tried to model myself on Kenji Midori, who won the fifth World Championship in 1991 at 72 kilos (158 lbs.) and 5'5". He didn't fight in a single tournament the year before that World Championship, and I had heard he did a huge amount of weight training to strengthen himself so he could compete against fighters much taller and heavier than himself.

If you watch old footage of him in that world tournament,

he stands toe-to-toe with guys a foot taller than him and 20 kilos heavier. Unlike other smaller fighters like Gary O'Neill, who moved around the bigger fighters to try to outpoint them (or, in the case of Gary, knock their heads off with one of his famous high kicks), Midori just beat all these famous guys on pure strength and power. He beat Masuda in the final, who weighed 87 kilos and looked like a giant standing next to him. In the first round, Masuda pushed Midori back. But in the second and third rounds, Midori actually stood toe-to-toe, often smashing Masuda into the other corner of the mat. He eventually won on the weigh-off (contestants get on the scales and if there is a 10 kilos difference, the lighter fighter wins) and shocked the karate world that had previously been dominated by heavyweights.

The craziness of 1995 wasn't confined to just what was happening in my world. On March 20, 1995, two months after the Kobe earthquake, there was a sarin gas attack on the Tokyo subway system. The cowardly attack was perpetrated by a religious cult called Aum Shinrikyo, which was run by a doomsday nutcase named Shoko Asahara. Sarin is a terrible weapon of destruction. Odorless and tasteless in liquid form, it turns to toxic gas when exposed to the air.

The cult members launched their attack on five subway trains at the peak hour of the morning, including our local train that passed through Nakano Sakaue Station. I remember going to the station that same morning, not knowing about the terrorist attack, and being told by police to catch a taxi. Of course, I was shocked and saddened by the news like everyone else in Japan.

Gas Panic

But I also couldn't help but wondering, what if I had gone to the subway station an hour or so earlier that morning?

In all, thirteen people died immediately from the gassing, and thousands more were poisoned and paralyzed for life. I often wonder what the real death toll was, if you count all the people who died in the hospital years later? It was definitely a crazy time in Tokyo…but little did I know that things would soon be getting crazier in the karate world, too.

CHAPTER 6: POLITICS

浪人

"We in Kyokushin maintain faith in the Way that knows no prejudices."

–Mas Oyama

Sosai's passing signaled the beginning of the end for the brotherhood of Australian Kyokushin, and Kyokushin worldwide. I arrived in Australia in August 1995 for the Australian Nationals, run by Shihan Jim Phillips. I was very surprised to see the number of high-level *Kyokushin* elite present, including Kenji Midori, Howard Collins, Kenji Sampei, and Akira Masuda. There had to be a reason for such big names to all be together in Australia at the same time, and I soon found out why: they were there to tell us that they were forming a breakaway group called Shin *Kyokushin*. Right away, they started giving fighters an ultimatum.

I almost felt betrayed by them. They were asking all of us – who had trained together for 20 years – to choose sides and therefore make enemies. *Kyokushin* broke up overpower, ego, money, and greed. I didn't care about gender, color, creed, or religion: if you were prepared to put on a *dogi* and come and train, we were on equal footing – and you earned my respect.

Shihan Eddie's dojo was with Matsui, and I was under Shihan Eddie in Australia, so I stayed in Matsui's group.

One clear memory is that Midori brought one of his young guns to compete, Kou Tanigawa, who I had fought twice in Japan and who later went on to become a two-time Shin *Kyokushin* World Champion. He was about the same age as me, and I remember having a friendly conversation with him. How strange life is. If only we had a crystal ball, maybe all these troubles could have been stopped somehow.

I fought in the heavyweight division of the last-ever unified *Kyokushin* karate Australian Nationals and was beaten on points by Papua New Guinean Walter (Wally) Schnaubelt. But the top two qualified for the Matsui World Tournament in October, so I spent an additional six weeks in Australia preparing for it, trying my best to ignore all the politics that were consuming *Kyokushin* karate.

I returned to Japan in October and fought in the 1995 World Tournament. I did reasonably well, thanks to my preparation. I was strong from all the heavy weight training, and my last six weeks of conditioning preparation were intense. But there were still fighters out there who had put in an overall harder year of training than me. I ended up making the top 32, and only lost in the fourth round after drawing with my opponent after two extensions. Both of us being of similar weight, it came down to the boards we broke at the beginning of the third day of the tournament. I ended up losing 22 to 21 (a combination of four different board breaks: elbow, knife hand, heel, and fist). If I had won this fight, my next opponent would have been my *Kyokushin* brother, Nicholas Pettas.

After the 1995 World Tournament, I stayed about one more year in Japan, working at a huge $50 million nightclub built by Avex Trax called Velfarre.

When I left Gas Panic to work at Velfarre, I ended up working with some of the guys from the *Honbu* Dojo. This is pretty interesting: my new workmates were Sugimura Senpai (the Razorback) and Ishida Senpai (the Barber), who were my senpais (seniors) at the *Honbu* Dojo. Nick was also supposed to work with us but declined at the last moment. He was one of the head instructors at *Honbu* and just wanted to concentrate on fighting without any outside distractions. But at Velfarre, my once-rivals were now my close work mates.

Sugimura Senpai finished 5th in the All-Japan tournament, beating the legendary Kurosawa Hiroki. Sugimura was without a doubt one of the strongest fighters in Japan, if not the world at this particular time. Nick and the Razorback were training partners and they were taking their training to another level. Velfarre was very clever to hire Kyokushin fighters for security. They had mainly a Japanese crowd, so there was hardly any trouble compared to Gas Panic. Velfarre even banned Yakuza from entering the club. But once in a while, some Yakuza would try to muscle their way in. However, as soon as they saw Sugimura standing there, their demeanor changed. Yes, even the Yakuza were big fans of *Kyokushin* and K1 fighters and paid their respect!

Anton, Nick, and Mike went to Europe, and Joe headed back to Australia in 1996, so I was feeling a bit lost and unsure of what direction I was going. I decided that I, too, would return to Australia. I missed my family and friends, and thought it was time to go home. With Sosai passing away, my feelings had changed about going to the *Honbu* dojo. Without Sosai there, I felt an emptiness and loneliness for him. He was the only reason for me to be in Japan in the first place. So, I packed everything up and returned to Oz.

I was so happy to see my family, but a lot of my closest friends ended up staying on or going back to live in Japan. Anton, especially, returned to Japan after Europe and ended up living there for 16 years. He started his own car export company, one of the first foreigners to ever do so without a Japanese partner. His company became one of the biggest suppliers of Japanese export cars to a number of different countries around the world. He used to tell me that every time a new sequel of *The Fast and Furious* movies came out, his sales spiked 30 percent!

Joe, too, had left Japan and come back to Australia. He missed his family and became wary of the dangers of the job. One day, he went to see Jackie Chan give a demonstration at a shopping center

Politics

in Melbourne. I remember he told me afterward he went up to the stage and thanked Jackie for the demonstration, and then asked him if he could give his own. Jackie said, "No problem," and Joe did his demonstration, and gave him one of his business cards. A week later he got a call from Jackie's manager, who asked Joe to play a bad guy role in a movie they were shooting in Sydney, *Mr. Nice Guy*. He ended up starring in three martial arts movies, always playing the bad guy.

He also starred alongside Jet Li in *Once Upon a Time in China and America*. After the first movie, Joe moved to America to pursue his Hollywood dream, opening two kung fu schools in LA and teaching martial arts to the stars. He ended up marrying the American girl of his dreams and had two kids, returning to Australia after about ten years in LA.

Arriving back in Australia, I remember lying in bed at night, thinking, "What am I supposed to do with my life?" I wished Sosai was still alive and dreamed about going back into the dormitory as a head instructor, living the simpler life I'd lived before. The *dojos* around the world were growing increasingly political and separating from each other, even writing each other threatening legal letters. Teachers and friends who had been close for many years were now being forced to choose between organizations. Depending on which group they chose, they weren't allowed to associate with any other group. How crazy is that? I couldn't believe what was happening.

Sosai would often say in class, and especially at camps, that when he passed away, he expected the seniors to stick together. He wanted everybody to work together, keeping *Kyokushin* one big family, one organization. He said this often, making his wishes clear. Sosai would look around the room, gazing into the eyes of his head instructors and say, "I'm depending and relying on you to keep it together." All the branch chiefs and teachers there would all yell *"Osu"* very loudly. How sad that this didn›t happen.

Sosai Oyama was such a powerful, kind, and unifying leader. He ruled an organization with some very strong personalities with an iron fist, and I guess no one could ever replace this great man.

People often ask me, "What do you think Sosai would say about what has happened to *Kyokushin* karate?" When I pause, the person who asked usually answers themselves, saying, "He would be rolling in his grave, wouldn't he?" I look at them and nod, not feeling comfortable with saying those words. But I do agree.

To this day, politics, power plays, and infighting still exist. It's a terrible shame because it's the students who miss out. They are held back, and when you're young and hungry, all you care about is training, learning, and bettering your life. You don't need these negative thoughts in your mind, hindering your progress and dreams. There is no room for ego, selfishness, arrogance, or boastfulness in karate. In fact, this applies not only in karate, but in human relations in general and everyday life. There's nothing wrong with being confident and standing up for what you believe in - but do it with humility. That's true leadership.

Sosai's words encouraged us to keep our heads bowed low, but eyes peered upward toward the sky. You were to be reserved in speech but have an indomitable fighting spirit. These are Sosai's teachings. Be kind to everyone and create peace. Karate starts with respect and ends with respect. That's why we bow to each other at the start of class and bow again at the end of class.

This is the path we, the Young Lions, were taught to take in life. And I pledged never to abandon that lesson.

CHAPTER 7:
THE RONIN YEARS, 1996-2006

浪人

"I realized that perseverance and step-by-step progress are the only ways to reach a goal along a chosen path."

–Mas Oyama

After arriving back in Australia in late 1996, I freely admit that I was lost. The bitter infighting among the branch chiefs and the death of my master had a huge impact on the direction – or, more accurately, the lack of direction – my life then took.

In ancient Japan, I might have been called a *ronin* – a wandering samurai with no lord or master. Under that nation's feudal system, a ronin was a samurai who had renounced his clan. Or it might be a samurai who had been discharged or ostracized, who had become a wanderer and stripped of their authority. The term ronin is synonymous with an outcast, an outlaw, a lordless samurai – especially one whose feudal lord had been deprived of his territory.

Although I wasn't literally wandering the countryside in Australia, looking back now, it seems an appropriate comparison to describe what I was going through. I had spent my formative years in Japan, and I have kept many of those Japanese traits and characteristics I learned in my *uchi deshi* days, so it certainly makes up a large part of my personality and outlook on life.

I wasn't sure where to train at first, so I took up a couple of different teaching positions before finally settling at Melbourne *Kyokushin* karate (MKK) under Shihan George Kolovos. I liked George because he was independent and non-political. I took classes four days a week and taught a Friday night fight class. Fighters would travel from all parts of Melbourne and Victoria to train with me on Fridays. I guess they all understood and appreciated that I wasn't political, either, and welcomed everyone to come and train. I stayed with George for about eight years.

George's background was *Kyokushin* karate, and he rented two vaults (warehouses) under Flinders Street Station to house his inner-city gym in those days. He always had his finger on the pulse of what the after-work city crowd wanted. In the early days it was Boxersize, and later on, it may have been Muay Thai. Whatever the public wanted, he offered it. Perhaps a lot of the city workers had seen *Fight Club* in those days, but whatever he taught, it was popular at the time, and he did very well financially. He was also a big fight promoter and organizer, and to this day, he still holds some every respectably sized Muay Thai and mixed martial arts nights.

I also started doing security work at a nightclub that was a Melbourne institution called the Chevron. I met some great people and friends for life while working there, people with whom I still stay in close contact, including Paul Phillips, Ned Vrselja and Costa Chondras. Ned, Michael Dugina, and Costa taught me a lot about boxing, and we trained a few days a week together in a makeshift gym we called "the House of Pain." They were top guys, and we sure trained hard as hell.

I loved training at the House of Pain and teaching at George's was going well, too. I fought in the Australian Nationals in 1995, 1996, and 1997. The last two were under the Matsui group, and I was beaten by the better fighter each time, Walter Schnaubelt (Wally), the nephew of the former PNG Prime Minister of 25 years, Michael Somare.

People who watched these tournaments say it was a golden era for Australian *Kyokushin* karate. The Australian Nationals were always held at the Sydney Town Hall, and there was always a big crowd and a lot of competitors. It was before *Kyokushin* really splintered over politics.

I weighed about 88 kilos and Wally was 100 kilos, and I was always a little banged up by the time I came to the final. It seemed I was always carrying some hurt in my legs or shins – as everyone who fights in those tournaments does. But then to face Wally, the 100-kilo monster, in the final bout certainly didn't make it easy for me. When I sparred with him in the dojo, we always seemed to be more evenly matched. But that said, he fought a lot of hard fights in the nationals, too, and I give credit where credit is due. He was the champion, and I was the runner-up.

I met Wally for the first time in 1991 at the fifth World Tournament. He had trained with Gary O'Neil as an *uchi deshi* of Cameron Quinn in Brisbane, at the same time as I had trained under Sosai (from 1990 to 1993). I knew Cameron from when he came down for his gradings under Shihan Eddie. For example, when he was going for his third *dan*, I was going for my first *dan*. Wally was about four years older than me, about 6'1" and 100 kilos. He was a powerful fighter, with great skill and incredible conditioning. He was also a funny, likable guy because he cracked jokes, was easy to talk to, and very passionate about his karate. He even stayed with us as an *uchi deshi* in Japan for about three months.

Wally, Nick, and I used to bash it out in the *Honbu dojo*, and I'm sure it helped all of us. He was a cool character, and later on, he even moved to Brazil to be an *uchi deshi* there. In 1993, he'd just lost to another future K1 legend, Francisco Filho, in the All-Brazil tournament. He also fought in Russia, and he told me fighting there was like a *Rocky* movie, only he was Rocky and everyone was cheering for Drago! I remember he came in second in that tournament, and also beat future K1 Champion Sam Greco in the Singapore tournament in 1992. Wally was a force to be reckoned with.

I met Cameron Quinn and Garry O'Neill, for the first time at the Elwood Dojo when I was 15 and Gary was 12. He came down to compete in the *Kata* competition, and he was a freak. He was talented, started young, and had a great teacher. He was a lightweight, about 70 kilos, and although he wasn't scared to stand toe-to-toe with anyone, he would use his angles and his timing with executing attacks was some of the best I've ever seen. He fought the great Japanese fighter, Kazumi, twice in the final in 1996 and 1997 All-Japan, and just barely lost. He was freaky in that he was so small, but such a smart fighter. His signature was a flying rollover spinning heel kick, which he used to knock out many fighters.

In 1998, Ralph Burd organized a big tournament at the Geelong Arena – Geelong always being a powerhouse of *Kyokushin* karate where the best fighters from all over Australia and overseas came to fight in a one-match challenge tournament. The draw card included me, Wally Schnaubelt, Gary O'Neil, Dominic Hopkins, Graeme Rose, and opposing fighters from Japan, Brazil, and New Zealand. I fought the reigning New Zealand Heavyweight Champion, Stephen Takiwa, and won by ippon with a spinning heel kick to the head.

This tournament attracted thousands, and in my eyes was the pinnacle of full-contact karate fighting in Australia. That same year, Wally, Garry, Dominic Hopkins, Richard Hood, and I also fought at the Coupe de Monde *Kyokushin* World Cup teams event held in Paris, France. Sixteen countries entered teams, and we made up the Oceania team. We ended up coming in third, after Japan and Brazil – a remarkable team effort.

George was a big city gym owner, and he also organized and promoted a lot of big karate-based fight events he called World Ring Karate. We had a good working relationship, and I fought a lot in his ring karate events. He brought fighters in from all around the world, mostly world-class *Kyokushin* fighters. Since it was ring karate and not a tournament, there was no need to get any political organization's okay. They were great events with huge crowds in those days, and I won all seven of my fights.

George managed me for a kickboxing fight in Japan at Korakuen Hall in 1999. I was inexperienced in this sport, and a long way from being properly prepared. I'd fought in a lot of his one-match karate fights and dominated but having trained for only four weeks in the lead-up, and now having to wear gloves and fight in a real ring, I just look back and shake my head. The Japanese guy I fought was a lot bigger than me and had something like a 30-0 fight record. He beat me with the three knock-down rules, literally giving me a big shove the third time to win.

This was a real wake-up call that I needed to work on my boxing skills, and it was about this time that I began training with Ned, Michael Dugina, Costa, Dan Causovski, and Glen Williams in the House of Pain. Dugina, being the Aussie rules Collingwood Football Club fitness coach, had ways of getting us fit like no other trainer I've ever met. He is amazing. Rowing machine, bikes, different kinds of interval running, pads, weights – it was a more modern, scientific way of getting fit. We trained twice a week, and I really think this complemented my karate training to an incredible degree. I have to say that these bi-weekly two-hour sessions were as hard as even the toughest of classes I ever experienced as an *uchi deshi* in Japan. After every training session we used to have a tradition of going to the local Nando's restaurant and eating up big while joking around, and this went on for at least five years from 1999 until about the year 2004. To this day, I still call Dugina and ask him about training tips and advice.

Ned owned and built our makeshift gym, and he was like a big cave man. He is gentle at heart but has the fighting spirit of a lion. I looked up to these guys a lot. They became my mentors. We used to train at Ned's Essendon gym near where I grew up twice a week on Tuesdays and Saturdays for many years.

They taught me a hell of a lot about boxing. In particular, they taught me about timing, ducking, weaving, footwork, moving the body to get maximum power and leverage, and all the stuff that *Kyokushin* never really taught – being a style that was more akin to standing toe-to-toe and slugging it out.

Glen was also part of the House of Pain, another joker not unlike Ned, but perhaps even on a grander scale. Also training with us regularly was Costa Chondras, who ended up winning the Australian Super Cruiserweight Championship in both the amateur and professional ranks at the same time. Ned and Dugina were Costa's boxing trainers. Costa was like the Mike Tyson of Australia, in my eyes. He was renowned for his power, a very exciting fighter, knocking out opponents in the majority of his fights with ten KOs in his thirteen wins. He had some of the hardest punches in the game, along with two of the best trainers in Ned and Dugina. But with boxing being what it is, he found it hard to find fights. Costa was such a nice and humble guy and really could have been the Champion of the World given the right manager and opportunity. But anyone who knows boxing knows that to get to that stage, you need more than skill alone. You also need a manager who is a master of wheeling, dealing, and politics.

It was a real honor to train with these guys. They were top mates, and we would hang crap on each other all the time, but we all had that same drive. We thought about training hard and doing the best we could.

I was still fighting in George's one-match challenges from 1998 to 2002, winning them all – most by knockout – against elite fighters from around the globe, including New Zealand, America, and Japan. This really gave me the boost of confidence I needed, seeing that I was still holding my own with some of the best while only training part-time. I often wondered how much better I would be if I could switch back to training full-time.

Outside of the World Cup team in Paris, I didn't fight often overseas, as the politics just made it too hard. The infighting at *Kyokushin* and how it was being torn apart prevented me from fighting more. In order to fight in any of the four different *Kyokushin* Karate World Tournaments, I would have had to pick a side and join one of their dojos. That meant not being able to teach at George's, fight in other non-affiliated tournaments, or

The Ronin Years, 1996-2006

train at other organizations' dojos. It also would mean that some of my students – who came from all over – would be told by their teachers that they could no longer train with me. So, I stayed neutral and satisfied myself with fighting ring fights and the odd independent tournament. I also stopped fighting in the Australian Nationals in 1998 because I was getting pressure from the Matsui group to join one of their dojos – even though, unofficially, I was still part of their group.

I felt in my heart a real sense of betrayal. But at the end of the day, it's up to you to stand up, be counted, and to lead your own way. After all, I was an *uchi deshi,* and we were expected to lead after we graduated, continuing Oyama›s legacy.

With all this in mind, and no real direction, I decided it was time to move on. I knew there was a new, exciting challenge out there waiting for me, and I wanted to find it.

Thailand was the answer. I began traveling to Thailand whenever I could save enough money, training for as long as I could stay. I'd go for two weeks up to three months, and I'd usually do a mixture of weights and any sort of martial arts I could find. Since it was Thailand, it almost always meant kickboxing or Muay Thai.

I enjoyed the lifestyle in Thailand; it was perfect for training. It had cheap food, cheap accommodation, cheap training, very happy-go-lucky people, and dedicated Muay Thai practitioners, so it really left an impression on me in those days.

As I said earlier, I supplemented my teaching income by

working at the Chevron nightclub and Esplanade Hotel for nightclub owners Paul and Vince Sofo. The Chevron was from 1996 to 2001, and the Espy from 2001 to 2004.

Our team was Ned, Costa, and me – talk about a mean team! We used to have a tradition of a huge feed at a local pizza joint, and then for 12 hours, work security with some of the baddest bad boys in Melbourne. Ned was always cracking jokes. Working such long hours in security, we all got along very well, and this helped pass the time. In 1996, the Chevron was renowned for university nights and $1 pints and people would get smashed so there were always a lot of fights. I remember the DJ particularly liked the song *"Eye of the Tiger,"* and I always used to shake my head when it came on, knowing that a fight was about to break out. These were mostly university students and the fights were harmless, so we'd usually just escort the young kids out who were just drunk on cheap spirits and beer.

The club around the corner, on the other hand, was a hardcore drug-taking trance joint named The Dome, populated with hardcore gangsters and renowned for shootings and stabbings. One time, two of the security officers got shot, so I guess we were lucky not to be working there.

One night, Ned and I were standing out in front of our club and we saw a scuffle happening between a man and a woman about 30 meters down from our front door. We proceeded to go down and take a look. When we got close, I remember the girl said to her companion, "pick up the picture," and he proceeded to pick something up. "Picture" must have been code since he picked up a handgun, which he pointed at Ned and me. He started yelling, "Get back, get back!" and swinging it from side to side. Out of the blue, we heard loud gunshots – perhaps two or three – coming from The Dome around the corner, shooting at this couple, who then took off running down St. Kilda Road. The next thing we saw was security from The Dome running down the street past us, shooting a massive gun at the couple. The girl stopped running, and the security guy ran past her and kept shooting at the guy – who spun around at regular intervals to return fire. But his gun was much smaller and sounded more like a cap gun in comparison. He then jumped in front of a car, hijacking it from a helpless driver before racing off!

We heard later that the couple had been knocked back from the front door of the venue, and then shot up the front of the club before running away. In the process, he dropped his gun halfway between the Dome and the Chevron entrance.

Looking back, I guess he probably thought we were security from The Dome. The funny thing was, I never saw or heard about this incident on the news, like it never happened. But then again, there was a huge underworld war going on in Melbourne in those days, so maybe this was just deemed a minor incident, not worthy of a headline.

The Chevron was a huge place with a different theme each night: one uni night, one gay night, and one big dance night. There was also a Croatian night where all the mad Croatians in Melbourne would come in and take the joint over. Can you imagine 500 huge Croatians walking around, drinking Slivovitz – their national firewater? These guys were monsters; it must be in their genes. And when they drink, they drink hard and like to fight. The only reason it worked was that Ned, too, was Croatian and a well-respected member of the Croatian community. Ned was as straight as an arrow and moonlighted doing security while he built up his fire door construction company. The Croatians all knew about Ned's boxing prowess and raw punching power, so if he told them to behave, they always apologized and changed tack immediately. Can you imagine all these seven-foot guys being told off by Ned, the scariest Croatian of all? It was a hilarious situation.

Security work in those days paid in cash and working with my mates was a lot of fun. But there are only so many days you can do something like that. They were great times, but the night shifts were taking their toll and I wasn't achieving what I had set out to achieve as a young kid. I wanted to be World Champion, and that desire never left me.

There was a big difference between living in Tokyo vs. Melbourne, where I had my own apartment and dated a number of girls. Later on, I settled down with my girlfriend, Jet Tranter, who lived with me from 2002 to 2006. She was an Aussie-Thai fitness freak with similar interests, and we got along well. Jet trained as a kick boxer, and even had a few professional fights before becoming a fitness model. More recently, she appeared in the film *Occupation Rainfall* in one of the main roles working beside some big names in Hollywood.

The press, and particularly *Blitz Magazine,* started to take notice of my ring fights. Since they were against big name opponents from countries around the world, including Japan, Brazil, and New Zealand, my fights always got a write-up. But they weren't national or world titles, and that was what I really wanted to win.

In the one-match challenges, I was fighting world-class fighters, but I wanted to win in Japan. I couldn't fight in *Kyokushin* tournaments outside of the *Kyokushin* Union because George was neutral, and so was *Kyokushin* Union under Shihan Hasegawa – who is a top bloke, and one of the true originals in *Kyokushin* karate. So, in 2002, I decided my next step was to win the World Championship in Japan. And there just happened to be a *Kyokushin* Union world Tournament that year, so I got on the plane with George and the Australian team and headed back to my former home.

CHAPTER 8: TAKING THE CHALLENGE BACK TO JAPAN

浪人

"Is it possible for even the smallest of accolades of achievement to be truly worthwhile without tears and toil?"

–Mas Oyama

2002 was the year the first *Kyokushin* Union World Championships were held in Shizuoka, Japan. The *Kyokushin* Union was a breakaway group – by this stage the fourth – and was run by Shihan Daigo Oishi and Shihan Kazuyuki Hasegawa, two very early *uchi deshi* and close students of Mas Oyama. Oishi Shihan came in fourth in the very first *Kyokushin* World Tournament, about which they made a movie called *The Strongest Karate*, showing him do a jumping flying side kick over an oncoming car.

Hasegawa Shihan came in third in the first tournament and

was champion in the second All-Japan championship. Both fighters are very well-respected leaders of *Kyokushin*. These two old-school leaders were also sick of the *Kyokushin* politics, so they decided to move away and create their own non-political organization in which anyone could fight. They were unique in that they didn't finger point or get involved in politics and – unlike the other organizations – they were truly non-political and would accept fighters and students to train in their dojos from any organization. This is, ultimately, why I chose to return to Japan and fight in their world tournament.

My girlfriend, Jet, and Anton (who was still living in Japan since our conversation over a game of golf in 1994) came along, too. Anton was on his way back from a business trip to Australia, so he flew on the same plane as George, Jet, all the other fighters from the Australian team and me. As I've told you, most of my friends left Japan in 1996, but Anton had a serious girlfriend and his large car export business. He was always present whenever I came to Japan to fight, so he probably knows my story better than anyone. Hence his role in my *100-Man Fight* documentary later on – and in this book itself.

I trained extremely hard for this tournament. Ned and Dugina had gotten me incredibly fit. As usual, to win the championship you needed to fight and win seven consecutive fights. I got through the first two quite easily, but the third fight was against a big Russian favorite and we really went to war. The fight went three rounds, and he got it on a very close decision. The corner referees judged it for two red flags and two white flags, but

Taking The Challenge Back To Japan

the center referee gave it to the Russian. I remember the center referee, Tabata Shihan, telling me at the sayonara party that he gave it to the Russian even though we were dead even, simply because I leaned over briefly at the end of the round rather than standing up straight and showing no weakness.

I felt upset, robbed, and let down because I had trained so hard. I remember thinking, "What am I doing wrong? Why can't I win, and what do I need to do to win?" I was extremely disappointed and totally in my own head for weeks about what I could do next to improve myself. I traveled with Jet, and I even remember arguing with her in the days before and after the tournament about really nothing at all. I decided that from that day forward, I would never have any distractions like that again in future tournaments.

When I got back to Australia, I stepped up my training even harder, fought in a few more ring karate tournaments organized by George, and decided at this stage it was time to give the Australian title another shot. So, in August 2002, back I went to face my nemesis at the Australian Nationals. It had been five years since I last took on this challenge and lost three times to the great Walter Schnabel. To move forward, this was a challenge I had to embrace and overcome.

I trained like a man on a mission, and when the day came – unlike at Shizuoka – everything went like clockwork. The only downside was that in the final, I had to fight one of my own students and training partners, Russ Sula, which was bittersweet.

He was a monster of a fighter, Albanian, tough as nails and could take and dish out punishment with the best of them. That said, there are no friends on the mat, only opponents, and when the fight started, we both got down to business. To be honest, it was a very strange situation. We fought tentatively for the first ten seconds, not really knowing how to react since we were such great mates and training partners. The ref immediately saw this, pulled us up, and asked, "You guys train together, don't you?"

We answered in the affirmative, and he gave us a quick dressing-down and said, "You've gotta ignore that. This is the final of the Australian National Championships, and it's your duty to go as hard as you can!"

So, from that moment on, we literally smashed each other, with the result being a decision for me in the first round. Finally, after all these years of trying and never giving up, I had won the Australian Heavyweight Championship. Russ and I regularly trained together at MKK, and we often smashed each other in the dojo, so it seemed fitting that we came first and second in the Australian Heavyweights that year. After all, he was another one of my brothers in arms.

I was elated about winning the Australian title. Even though I was disappointed that I hadn't done better in the *Kyokushin* Union World Championships, it gave me the taste for fighting back in Japan. In Shizuoka, although I lost early, it was the closest of decisions and I won the Fighting Spirit Award for the tournament. Now, having won the Australian Heavyweight title, I gained new confidence and realized that to take things to the next step meant winning in the home of karate – Japan. To me, the only way was to win an All Japan or, one step better, a World Championship. So, from 2002 onward, this became my sole mission in life.

My next foray into Japan was traveling with George, again as my manager, to Osaka in 2004, to fight in what was known as the Byakuren Karate World Championship, founded and run by the well-liked and respected Kancho Masayasu Sugihara. Byakuren is a full-contact karate style with tournament rules similar to *Kyokushin*. The standard of fighters in these tournaments is as good as can be found anywhere in the world.

Sugihara, like Hasegawa, was also non-political and he wanted the strongest fighters to battle it out in his tournament, so he invited fighters from many full-contact styles. I remember Ademir De Costa, a *Kyokushin* legend, being there. He, too, was someone who had completed the legendary 100-man *Kumite*.

George knew Sugihara Kancho through some smaller tournaments in Japan, and he was able to get a number of his strongest fighters a place in the tournament – including Russ, Phil Jacobson, Russell Frazier, Dwayne Harris, and me. That was a tough tournament, and I was given a very hard draw – as the Japanese often assigned to the foreign fighters. I remember fighting a tough American in the first round, and then Tadanobu Oue, a tough Japanese fighter I had fought before in the karate ring fights for my second matchup. There was a big Japanese guy in the third fight, and then I fought the reigning Byakuren champion and favorite, Minami, in the semi-final. The fight was well matched, and in the beginning, I came very close to taking his head off with at least two axe kicks. I remember missing by centimeters and thinking how close I came to stopping the fight right then and there. Then, not long after in that same first round, we got in close, exchanging a flurry of kicks and punches. But he swept me while also pulling me down by the *dogi* – technically an illegal move, but obviously not seen by the judges, so he was awarded a half point.

To understand how the point system works in full-contact karate: a full point, or *ippon*, is considered a knockout and is immediately the end of the fight. A half point, or *wazari*, means that unless the opposing fighter evens the score within that round, they will end up losing. So, I lost, and my dream to win the World Championship eluded me again.

In the final fight, Yuyu Kitajima became the first Byakuren Karate World Heavyweight Champion by knocking out Minami with an incredible knee strike to the chin. He is an incredible fighter and part of the younger generation, so this was a real changing of the guard. I was honored to be able to fight in the very first Byakuren World Championship, but quietly disappointed to come in third. I was training as hard as I had ever trained, had traveled a long distance to fight, and entered to win it all. But to do that, you must win up to seven fights in one day against the best in the world. There are no second chances, and there can be only one champion. Kitajima was champion, and my quest for a world championship title continued.

Taking The Challenge Back To Japan

In 2005, I entered what was known as the Abu Dhabi Full-Contact World Championship, and again I came in third. In the same year, I remember doing a kickboxing fight in one of George's shows, and I won the fight by decision. In early 2006 I entered and won the Victorian Heavyweight Championship, but really, I was thinking, "What I am doing here? I'm not moving forward; if anything, I'm moving backwards. I've fought some of the best in the world in George's ring tournaments, and I'm now regularly traveling to Japan for the world tournaments and fighting low-level kickboxing or state championships isn't moving me forward."

Something needed to change.

CHAPTER 9: MOVING TO THAILAND TO STEP UP THE FIGHT

浪人

"I have not permitted myself to be ignorant of any martial art that exists. Why? Such ignorance is a disgrace to someone who follows the path of martial arts."

–Mas Oyama

In 2006, I told George I'd decided to move to Thailand to train full-time and take it to the next level. Thailand is often called the mecca of fighting, and I had decided that living and training there full-time might just make the difference between placing in the top three and finally being number one.

At that stage of my career, I had an incredible desire to climb to the pinnacle in martial arts, and that meant winning the World Championship. In the *Kyokushin* World Union and Byakuren karate world tournaments, both times I'd proven myself a capable fighter, and from what the Japanese karate elders said to me as encouragement after the tournaments, I left a good impression. But, as appreciative as I was of their encouraging words, just leaving a good impression was not my aim. The competitive spirit in me meant that one day, I wanted to be the one standing on top of that dais. I often thought back to Sosai and his teachings, talking to us *uchi deshi* about one day becoming World Champions, and all these years later it was still my aim and the driving force in my life.

This competitive fire in my belly was still burning strong. But after those two big tournaments, seeds of doubt were planted in my head as to where my training might go if I stayed in Australia. I seemed to be stagnating, and perhaps the move to full-time training was the change I needed to win. I was already going to Thailand every few months on training missions, so moving there permanently seemed the logical next step in my career. So, I sold all my worldly belongings, including all of my furniture and my car, to chase my dream. I had also just separated from my girlfriend, Jet, so it was the perfect time to follow my heart and begin a new journey in life.

George gave me the name and address of a New Zealand teacher named Sifu Robert McInnes who was living in Pattaya, Thailand. Sifu Robert was also a Colonel in the Thai Army. So, from here on in the book, I'll refer to Sifu Robert as The Colonel. The Colonel ran a martial arts school, which at that time was called the South East Asian School of Martial Arts. Located in a four-level building on Sukhumvit Road, it was a hardcore training facility with Muay Thai on the top floor (including a full-sized ring and lots of heavy bags) and martial arts dojos on both the second and third floors.

The Colonel's style of training was totally unusual to me. He technically called it *Sir Gi Dor*, which is a Chinese version of Shaolin kung fu. The main training included a lot of break falls and weaponry, which I'd never done before, so I found it interesting. He taught all these different techniques that I'd never done before, such as kung fu style punches, throws, and take-downs, which don't exist at all in *Kyokushin*.

After only two months of training there, The Colonel offered me a job as a salesman for his apartment development company. For the next three years, that job gave me the income to pay my way in Thailand. Within three months, I was also offered a job as an instructor at the school. The Colonel had heard of me and my accomplishments, and obviously he knew of *Kyokushin* and the fact I was an *uchi deshi* of Mas Oyama. He wanted to really revolutionize the style of training at his school so that his younger students would become competitive in full-contact tournaments. With the type of training, he was offering when I first got there, that was never going to happen. So, to put it simply, you could say that I brought all of my *Kyokushin* and tournament fighting training with me and changed the whole style and concept of his school.

We spent at least half our time training purely on fighting and conditioning in the way I'd been trained over a lifetime. We also mixed it up with The Colonel's traditional teachings, but within three years, the training evolved even more toward my style of pure fight training.

The Colonel's dojo in Pattaya was a tight-knit family of trainers and local and visiting students, and they took their training seriously, whether it was in Muay Thai, kickboxing, or boxing, or any martial art. I was thrilled to be able to join them in my new role as head martial arts instructor, under The Colonel. However, I had no idea the ups and downs I would go through with The Colonel in the future.

CHAPTER 10: THE COLONEL

浪人

"In martial arts, introspection begets wisdom. Always see the contemplation of your actions as an opportunity to improve."

–Mas Oyama

The Colonel was clearly a father figure of the kung fu family, and his students loved his training. They would do anything he tells them. About 55 years of age at the time, The Colonel was an enigmatic, larger-than-life character who had a long history in martial arts. He'd lived in Thailand for 25 years, bringing his own style of martial arts. Although he's lived a life of adventure with more adventure than 100 normal lifetimes combined, he never let the truth get in the way of a good story! I'm sure if he ever sat down and wrote out his real-life story it would be a best seller, but that would mean sticking to the truth.

We do know that The Colonel first came to Pattaya about 25 years ago. There are rumors he sold hot dogs on Walking Street to begin with, and then moved on to building swimming pools and finally multi-story apartments as a major property developer. At the same time, he continued teaching his unique form of martial arts, as well as Muay Thai, the local fighting art. He has many pictures and memorabilia adorning the walls of his now world-class five-story gym, including pictures of some of those who have trained with or under him over the years. It really is a Who's Who of Thai fighting royalty. Famous figures include the legendary Muay Thai fighter Sakmongkol (who is still one of the main trainers at the WKO), as well as Ramon Dekker, Peter Aerts, Ernesto Hoost, Remy Bonjasky, Stan Longinidis, and Bobb Sapp, just to name a few.

When I arrived in Thailand, he was still in the old school on Sukhumvit Road. But he wanted to expand, so within 18 months of my beginning there, we moved to a five-story facility in Pattaya Klang – a huge main road in Pattaya. It consists of a reception area on the first floor, a weight training gym, two floors of dojo space, and the top floor with a full ring, bags, and huge area for Muay Thai and kickboxing training. The new school was a massive improvement over the old one. The old school was pretty basic – clean, but no air conditioning, and stifling during training because it was so hot it would be difficult to breathe. But the training sessions were tough, hard, and intense, and he was great at getting the best out of his students.

About six months into my tenure, The Colonel took me to one side and began to map out what I later realized was his master plan. This was in 2007. He called me over to his house one

The Colonel

morning and started asking me about the tournaments in Japan, picking my brain for ideas about traveling and even starting a dojo in Japan, as well as having his students fighting in full-contact tournaments. He felt me out about going over there and making this a reality. At this stage, The Colonel had been a cornerman for Peter Aerts in the Japanese K1, but really had zero experience in the karate tournament fighting system that I was familiar with for most of my life. He wanted to start an organization called the World Kumite Organization (WKO), so the new school was plastered in massive banners, signs, and a new logo across the top of the building reflecting this change.

It was around this time that The Colonel told me he wanted to alter the style of training at his school, turning his students into world-class full-contact karate tournament fighters. This was not going to be an easy task. Imagine, for example, his style of *Sir Gee Dor*, being what it was, probably a very effective style of martial arts, but certainly not suited to the sort of toe-to-toe slugfests that full-contact tournaments were becoming famous for. I knew, however, that I had a great foundation at the school, as the one thing that The Colonel's students were not lacking was ambition and fighting spirit. This was obviously instilled in them by The Colonel and his training from an early age. So, in my mind, all I needed to do was to teach them what I had learned as a youth in Japan, preparing them as much as possible to compete in extremely tough Japanese tournaments.

Even before we moved to our new headquarters, I found myself teaching classes in conjunction with The Colonel and, most importantly, taking all the fighting classes. This involved a lot of technical training, such as fighting combinations, how to block and check kicks correctly, how to counter fight, required fighting combinations, and giving the students a general understanding of a fight plan and how to win.

All the kids had great technique and kicks, and they were strong and fit. But it's a totally different thing to integrate those skills into a successful fighting game plan that will win them a tournament match. Since they all had such a great attitude, they adapted quickly, and I was proud and happy to be working with them.

I found a new home at the WKO *Honbu* in Thailand. I was training every day, usually twice a day, and really enjoyed the lifestyle. We had a great bunch of trainers and students, all very dedicated, and some serious emerging talent as well.

The Colonel was a major part of me stepping up my training from 2006 onward. Between winning the Australian Nationals and then placing third in two consecutive World Tournaments, I was becoming more and more confident that I could hold my own with the best in the world. Like everyone else, I felt down at times, devastated by decisions that were so close, but that didn't last long after the tournaments were over. As one of Mas Oyama's Young Lions, I was taught to *gaman suru* – to persevere, to fight through self-doubt and never give up.

In order to get there, The Colonel and his school in Thailand were the perfect fit for me. With him and his school, I could step

The Colonel

up my training and have the best chance to succeed at my dream.

I've talked a lot about *budoka*, the relationship between a martial artist and his master. I've always said that Sosai Oyama was my only master, and if I am being truly honest with myself, this really is the case. I'm not detracting from The Colonel one bit by saying this. He is a very accomplished martial artist and a drill sergeant with no equal. If there's ever someone who needs to be trained within an inch of their life, I would happily recommend The Colonel to get them into shape. He has this ability to push people to their ultimate physical and mental limits and get the best out of them. However, at this stage in my career, I really think we were peers in terms of martial arts knowledge and training. I was key, I believe, in turning his school from a traditional Shaolin Monk kung fu-based martial art of basic techniques, rolls, grabs, and weaponry into a full-contact, stand-up, tournament-ready school of fighters. In return, The Colonel gave me the opportunity to teach and train full-time so I could make a living and achieve my dream of being a World Champion. I was – and still am - very thankful for that.

One day, I would be World Champion, I reminded myself. I swore that all the lessons and training Sosai instilled in me as a young man would not be in vain. One day, I was going to win the ultimate test. I just didn't know then that the ultimate test was not necessarily a World Championship, but something far more ambitious and difficult.

CHAPTER 11: THE WKO FAMILY

浪人

"Karate is budo and if budo is removed from karate it is nothing more than sport karate, show karate, or even fashion karate – the idea of training merely to be fashionable."

–Mas Oyama

Moving to Thailand changed my whole life. I left everyone I'd known behind for the third time, sacrificing my comfortable, familiar existence to chase my dream. But in Thailand, I met some incredible new people who would become my friends for life who worked and trained at the WKO *Honbu*.

Nick Kara is a former kickboxing champion and comes from a Muay Thai background. He was from Melbourne, just like me, and came to Thailand at a young age to learn art under different teachers. When I met him, he was about 35 and The Colonel was his trainer. Nick had actually just finished starring as one of the bad guys in a cult Thai martial arts movie called *Ong-Bak* that also became a hit overseas. This movie really kicked off Tony Jaa's career, who is now starring in Hollywood movies such as *The Fast and The Furious 7* and *Skin Trade*.

Nick is a very muscular, chiseled, and intimidating character. He just looks big and mean, covered in tattoos, with a large forehead, and protruding jaw. Even his face has muscles! He's the spitting image of Mickey Rourke's character, Marv, from Sin City – in both looks and demeanor. But despite his intimidating appearance, once you get to know Nick, he's an incredibly decent and loyal person, second to none. I guess we all battle our demons at some stage or another, but Nick seemed to wear his heart on his sleeve. His fight name was Special K, and he had so many tattoos he put Max Cady from *Cape Fear* to shame. I had to laugh when I asked him about the particularly fascinating tattoos he had on the inside of each wrist, the ace from a deck of cards. Nick's response was that he always had an ace up each sleeve!

That said, Nick is without a doubt one of the most gifted boxing and kickboxing trainers I have ever met. He has this uncanny ability to watch someone box for 15 to 30 seconds and immediately recognize – and fix – what they are doing wrong, whether it's incorrect footwork, timing, balance, head movement, or just about anything else in the boxing playbook. He is, for lack of a better phrase, a star in the world of kickboxing training, and I was incredibly fortunate to have him in my corner in many of my fights from there on in.

Sakmongkol Sithchuchok is the head Muay Thai trainer at

The Wko Family

WKO. A former professional Muay Thai fighter, he's an absolute legend in the sport and famous all around the world. Sakmongkol is known as one of the most iconic Muay Thai fighters of all time, fighting in the super middleweight division and defeating other Muay Thai greats such as Ramon Dekkers, Danny Bill, Perry Ubeda, John Wayne Parr, Jongsanan Fairtex, and many others. His record stands at an incredible 231 wins, 4 draws, and 19 losses.

Sakmongkol is a five-time WMC World Champion and a three-time Lumpinee Stadium Champion in the 1990s, the Muay Thai "Golden Era." Known for his devastating left kicks and tough body conditioning, he could take a lot of punishment and still push the fight forward. He started training at just six years old and had his first fight when he was eight. He then made it to Lumpinee Stadium at the age of 12, which is like the mecca of Muay Thai fighting (and gambling!). At 18, he fought and defeated the Dutch legend, Rammon Dekkers at Lumpinee. His most famous battles, a total of seven fights, were against Jongsanan Fairtex. Their fifth fight became known as the "Elbow Fight," and is considered one of the most brutal and best Muay Thai fights of all time, with both fighters drenched in blood and barely conscious when the fight concluded.

Mong, as Sakmongkol is affectionately known at the gym, will always be an absolute superhuman freak of nature in my mind. He's tall for a Thai, and thin and wiry like most Thai boxers. He has this incredible will and determination, and nothing will ever stand in the way of his quest. He ran 21 kilometers a day, six days a week, as well as training Muay Thai every day in the gym! And all he ever eats is Magi noodle soup, a brand of instant noodles from 7-11. He is simply not human!

Mong is quiet and keeps mostly to himself, but he has this steely, primal look in his eyes that flashes during a fight. He has eyes like those of a wild tiger, burning with the joy of victory. Fighting is what he was built to do. He is a proud man, a loyal person, and has been working with The Colonel since about the time he retired from professional Muay Thai fighting.

I remember thinking once that I should try to introduce Mong to a protein shake after training, something that was a staple for me. My diet included loads of protein, meat, and vegetables – something I honed and perfected to suit my body so I could withstand my intense daily workouts. But, after a little consideration, I thought, *"why mess with someone who has lived on cup-of-noodles for 30 years and has won 230 out of 250 fights?"*

Maybe eating meat, vegetables, and protein is not right for this type of superman. His system of training and eating has worked for 40 years, so why tinker with this impeccable machine?

Thai fighters are so strong because they literally fight to feed their families. In Western society, we have a roof over our heads, food on the table, and all the creature comforts and luxuries are accessible to us.

But the Thais fight just to survive. Can you imagine that mindset? For me, Thais are the strongest pound-for-pound fighters in the world. True warriors understand that their one and only job is to decimate the opponent in front of them. They may be smaller in stature (the average Thai fighter is only about 160 cm, or 5'2, and 55 kilos, which is 122 pounds!), but they have heart like no other. Thais have an incredible amount of confidence. Remember that Thailand is the only Southeast Asian country never to have been conquered or colonized. That protect-what's-ours-or-die spirit comes out in their fighting.

In most countries, professional fighters are ripped with muscles, shoot their mouths off to self-promote, and walk around with an entourage. But Thai fighters are so placid in nature that you won't even realize they're fighters. I think it has to do with Buddhism and their beautiful, serene culture.

They also start fighting – not just training - from a very young age, sometimes as early as six or seven. Poor parents will send a boy who shows promise to a Muay Thai academy, where he might earn his keep by cleaning. Some of these boys sleep right in the ring at night with kick pads as pillows.

It's survive or die. Thai fighters take an incredible amount of abuse until they have no nerve endings left in their shins and legs, using them like steel blades. Thais also fight a lot, sometimes 200-400 times in a career. There's no six-month training camp leading up to a fight, and the fledgling professionals who are trying to rise up in the ranks (and earn enough for their families to eat) may get a call that they're needed for a fight in a few hours, or that night. They can't say no to a fight because their families depend on them.

Western fighters have a lot to learn from the Thais. Whether they are practitioners of *Kyokushin* karate, boxing, MMA, or Muay Thai, Westerners who want to improve in their skill and toughness often travel to Thailand to get out of their comfort zones.

With Thailand's humidity and hot weather, the gains in endurance and conditioning are huge – it's akin training in high altitude. The heat really zaps your energy and takes some getting used to, and you won't find air conditioning inside Muay Thai gyms, many of which are outdoors. No wonder the Thais are so strong and fit! Sakmongkol is a product of this and a true living legend, and it was an incredible honor to work beside him for so many years.

Mohammad, or Double Tap (DT) as he is known, was my closest ally at the WKO gym and main training partner along with Nick Kara. I first saw DT fight in the WKO World Championship in 2008. With a *Kyokushin* background, and many times the Iranian National Champion, he came in third in the World Championship and left quite an impression. He returned about three months before the 2010 WKO World Championships to train and prepare at the *Honbu*. Again, he came in third, after which The Colonel offered him a position as an assistant teacher.

He was initially shy and didn't speak much English. But DT was polite, humble, trained extremely hard, and was as tough as nails. He has this signature move that I've never seen anywhere else in the world. We called this move – and, by extension, him – the Double Tap. This move involves a double kick: a right kick to either the thigh or the body, followed immediately by a left kick to the head with devastating effects. The opponent, having leaned in or flinched due to the impact of the first kick, dropping his guard due to the power of Mohammad's kick, never expected a left kick to the head immediately, especially before DT's right foot even touches the ground. Essentially, he was airborne throughout the entire sequence.

DT became world renowned for this signature move and knocked out so many fighters with his deadly weapon. He fought as a lightweight at 70 kilos, but he often chose instead to fight in the heavyweight divisions and won, like when he won the heavyweight division of the All-Okinawa Open karate tournament, one of the most prestigious tournaments in Japan. Being such a nice guy, he was loved by all at the WKO and quickly became a member of the close-knit WKO family.

I became very close friends with DT. We not only trained together, but we also used to have what we called our Friday night traditions where we would have a few beers or a little local Samsung whiskey and then hit the town. Sometimes, we went a little bit overboard! But that was always outside the times of competition – during which I religiously abstained from anything but training, eating, and sleeping for at least six weeks in the lead up.

There were other trainers at WKO, too, including Mutt – another Muay Thai trainer – and Christina, a martial arts trainer. Christina, along with Olivia, Pim, Stephanie, Minto, Isabella, and Noot made up a team of girls at the school I nicknamed the Kill

Bill Girls after the Quentin Tarantino movie. All were young and beautiful, and all were black belts, highly skilled and dedicated martial artists.

On her own, or sometimes with all the girls as a team, Christina would often perform demonstrations at local tournaments or in Japan with weapons and staffs. They were simply incredible to watch in action. By the time I'd been there for a couple of years, a few of them had become competitive tournament fighters – especially Minto and Isabella. Minto won a major regional Byakuren tournament against the best in Japan for her age group. All of them are half Thai and mesmerizingly beautiful. Pim, particularly, is now a famous Thai supermodel, and can be seen on the cover of Thai *Vogue* every other month.

The martial arts classes grew in numbers after we moved to the new school. We were evolving the teaching and training of martial arts there, taking the best parts from every style and using it in its most effective way to fight better in traditional full-contact tournaments. The school quickly grew a reputation for excellence, and The Colonel began inviting karate instructors from around the world to come train and join his WKO.

In the Muay Thai gym upstairs, there was also a mix of locals and foreigners visiting from overseas. Professional fighters often came and spent a month or more training under Mong, Nick Kara, DT, and myself to prepare themselves for upcoming fights. Mong and Nick Kara took care of the kickboxing, and DT and I took on the full-contact fighting and body conditioning. The Colonel was, as always, the motivator and drill sergeant from hell.

We welcomed fighters from all different styles to come and join our dojo, and The Colonel would often ask specialists from other styles to take the class. Cris Brown, a famous Australian five-time Olympic wrestler, used to come and bring his fighters to improve their stand-up while teaching us wrestling techniques from his 30 years of experience. We had a small group of Brazilian jiu-jitsu practitioners come in twice a week, and I tried to attend their sessions on days when we didn't have the martial arts class.

There were too many great students at the school for me to mention them all (TK, Christina, Peter, and Noiy all deserve a shout out), but it was an incredible time, and I was very happy to be training and teaching there, surrounded by people who enjoyed martial arts as much as I did. I was doing what I was born to do and felt a part of the WKO family.

Many of the students had been training since they were little kids, and were all well-spoken, polite, and disciplined. This is what martial arts does for people, and it was a pleasure to teach these kids. I say "kids," since the adult class was ages twelve and up. By that time, I was hitting my mid-30s, so even the young adults seemed like kids to me!

They were yet another reminder that the clock was ticking. It was time for me to step it up if I wanted to achieve my ultimate goal: to honor Sosai's legacy.

CHAPTER 12: KANCHO SUGIHARA AND THE RISE OF THE WKO

浪人

"A man who understands decorum and to be courteous is a great treasure; I hope to train and send into society as many such men as I can."

–Mas Oyama

In 2007, I traveled once again to Japan, this time with The Colonel and a group of ten of his students to fight in Shihan Hasegawa's regional Nagano Tournament. In addition to me, there was TK, the Kill Bill Girls, Christina, and a lot of the young up-and-coming students from the Thai school. I was there in a coaching role, and this was their first time in Japan to attend a karate tournament, so I also acted as translator and advisor. It was a great experience for The Colonel and the kids, and I'm sure having The Colonel's own son, Robert Junior, fighting at the age of ten made him very proud. That tournament really opened up his eyes to the standard and intensity of fighting in Japan, even though this was just a regional tournament. The whole Japanese spirit, organization, and everything involved in the tournament really blew The Colonel away.

Not long after this tournament and our trip to Japan, The Colonel came up with the idea of a worldwide non-political organization that would encompass all styles under one umbrella, allowing them to fight each other in officially sanctioned tournaments with typical full-contact karate rules. Basically, the same as *Kyokushin*. In order to do this, he needed two things: contacts in the Japanese karate world (where I still had good standing as did George Kolovos and Shihan Eddie), and also letters of introduction. My best mate, Anton, who was still running his company in Tokyo, had his staff translate those letters.

But the real key to all of this was Kancho Masayasu Sugihara. As I mentioned earlier, Kancho Sugihara was the head of the Byakuren karate Organization at the time, with its *Honbu* base in Osaka. Finding history in English on Sugihara Kancho is not easy, but there are mentions of him starting his martial arts career in Shorinji Kempo under the founder So Doshin and achieving his sixth *dan* by the age of 28 – quite an incredible feat.

The legend goes that he was the personal bodyguard of So Doshin until his death. There are references to So Doshin being a formidable character who quarreled with local Yakuza bosses, so perhaps this explains his need for a bodyguard. In any case,

Kancho Sugihara And The Rise Of The Wko

after So Doshin passed away, it is said that Shorinji changed direction toward non-contact and non-competition, so Sugihara Kancho left and founded his own style in 1984, calling it *Byakuren* karate.

Kancho Sugihara was always charismatic, loved by all in Byakuren Karate across Japan. His organization is non-political, so he allowed me to fight in many of his tournaments as an equal amongst his own students and competitors. Kancho is renowned for going around in a blue kimono, wearing tinted eyeglasses and a gold watch hanging around his neck. Outside of his martial arts prowess and movie-star eccentricities, he is also a talented singer, releasing a Japanese enka recording to great local acclaim.

Byakuren karate is huge in Japan. They hold yearly All Japan Tournaments, and a World Tournament every four years. Their tournaments are held in the Osaka Prefectural Stadium, and the Byakuren *Honbu* is not far away in Osaka as well. I was amazed and impressed with Byakuren karate's kids' tournaments, which are also held once a year. Over 1,000 kids from more than 100 different styles compete together under the same set of full-contact karate rules, all in one day. What's even more amazing is that it starts at precisely 10 a.m. and finishes at 4 p.m. Only the Japanese could be this organized.

These kids tournaments really are something to behold, bigger and better organized than anything I've seen anywhere in the world. There are ten mats going at the same time, with kids from 5 to 17 years old, and all open weight. Unlike in Australia, or even the *Karate Kid* movies – this is full-contact, no-holds-barred. The young kids are wrapped up in protective gear like the Michelin Man. But as they get older, most of the protective gear is removed and it gets closer to what the adults are doing in their tournaments. The standard, I can say without a doubt, is second to none.

So, Kancho Sugihara – with an already large organization, his iconic personality, and ability to bring people together – became an essential leader of the WKO. He renamed his tournaments Byakuren WKO and, along with Shihan Hasegawa, George, and Eddie, encouraged schools from different styles around the world, as far away as Australia, Africa, Iran, Brazil, Russia, and Thailand, to become a part of this umbrella organization. All of these nations and cultures fought in joint tournaments, sharing training techniques from around the world. There were no politics here; no infighting or arguments about who was boss and who could fight or train with whom. Anyone who trains in a full-contact style is welcome to join. Their best fighters are invited to fight in the WKO and affiliated tournaments.

Thus began the rise of the WKO, my long-term relationship with Byakuren karate, and friendship with the great Kancho Sugihara.

CHAPTER 13: NEVER GIVE UP

浪人

"If you have confidence in your own words, aspirations, thoughts, and actions, and do your very best, you will have no need to regret the outcome of what you do. Fear and trembling are the lot of the person who, while stinting effort, hopes that everything will come out precisely as he wants."

–Mas Oyama

My best mate Anton was diagnosed with cancer in early 2008. He'd come home from Japan to Australia for Christmas, as usual, but after Christmas lunch, was struck down with severe stomach pains and couldn't get up off the sofa. In early January, he visited a doctor and the prognosis wasn't good. The pain he'd been ignoring for more than a year was a tumor in his bowels. The doctor told him it was stage three, and most people don't come back from anything above two, so he'd better get his affairs in order.

Anton being so far away, I felt powerless to help. I'd already lost a good mate of the same name to suicide when I was a first year *uchi deshi*. How could Anton have cancer? He was indestructible. He was one of those guys who had that weird light around him, and you knew no matter what crazy risks he took in life, he wasn't going to get so much as a scratch.

Anton was there for me at every Japanese tournament I competed in. Every single one. He always came and cheered me on, no matter where it was held. If it wasn't in Tokyo, he'd get on the bullet train or drive to the tournament, either alone or sometimes with a couple of friends in tow. And it was because of me that he had spent most of his adult life living in Japan, where he worked hard and built up a wildly successful business.

I called him after his operation, and he told me that the doctors had cut out about a foot of his large intestine. Six months of chemotherapy was next. The doctors were worried that the cancer cells may have gotten into his blood, so they were going to zap him hard with the strongest chemo possible before it had the chance to spread elsewhere. Basically, they said because he was young and had such an aggressive cancer, they were going to try to poison him to the maximum limit, killing the cancer but stopping short of killing *him* in the process. He was told that he was going to be very sick from this treatment and wouldn't be able to do much.

I asked him how he was going to handle his business while having chemo in Australia, and he said it was no problem. He'd just fly to Japan and back to Australia every other week. Anton told me that when the doctor first gave him the dark prognosis, Anton told the doc to cheer up and not to pick out a coffin just yet.

That cheered me up. Typical Anton. Nothing fazed him. Incredibly, his sister Jackie (who was just two years older than him) had just beaten cancer herself – and one of the worst kinds: brain cancer. What a tragic coincidence. And Anton was planning to fly to and from Japan every second week for six months after chemo? What a crazy single-minded man - he was never, ever going to give up!

Anton's fighting spirit definitely inspired me, too. I continued training hard in Thailand, harder than I had ever trained before. The life of a full-time *karateka* was all I ever wanted. I was entering the top tournaments in the world, still trying to win that elusive world title. But no one in the fight world is ever an overnight success, and all the hard work and training still doesn't guarantee a World Championship.

I was now traveling from Thailand to Japan to fight in every major tournament that I could. I don't want to brag, but people always told me I was an exciting fighter. I had a lot of power in my punches and kicks from all the heavy weight training and I could take down fighters with my hard-hitting body shots. I also employed a lot of high kicks, which the crowd always loves to watch, and my signature moves were my axe kick and spinning heel kick, perfected all those years ago in the *Kyokushin Honbu*. They say you can tell a former *uchi deshi* from those high kicks, and countless thousands of repetitions had nearly perfected that part of my fight game.

I prepared for months in advance for these big tournaments. In the off-season, I did a huge amount of cross training and body conditioning to the point that I could take just about any punishment anyone in the world could dish out. All that strength and cardio training meant that I would never gas out as I punched and kicked like a bull. Six weeks out, I would live like a monk, concentrating only on the build-up to the match day with just one aim in mind. I had almost perfected how to time my training so that, come fight day, I would be jumping out of my skin.

In August 2008, I entered the heavyweight division of the inaugural WKO World Tournament held in Thailand. The best fighters were invited from all over the world, and I trained as hard as I ever had for this one. I got to the final against Amirhamzeh Fathi, the Iranian champion, and felt like I was controlling the fight and well ahead. Then, just 30 seconds from the end, he did a rolling axe kick, which he was famous for, and knocked me out. I was 30 seconds away from achieving my dream when Fathi snatched victory away from me. He deserved to win, but again I couldn't help but feel gutted. My good mate, Russ, came 4th and Mong finished best eight in the middle weight division. Russ, my dedicated training partner, fought some incredibly strong opponents that day and I couldn't be prouder.

In November of the same year, I entered the second Byakuren World Tournament in Osaka, Japan. Anton had completed his chemo, and although he wasn't in the greatest shape, he came back to Japan and supported me as he always did. This time I got to the semi-final against Paulinho Barros from Portugal. There was a bit of grabbing on both sides when we were close, but for some reason the judges decided to award a *genten*, or half point, against me. So, in order to win, I had to knock him out or at least get a half point back. I really stepped it up and smashed his legs with some of the hardest kicks I could muster, but to no avail. At the end of the fight, he was battered but still standing and was awarded the win. In the final he fought the reigning champion, Kitajima, and buckled after about 30 seconds. You could say Kitajima should thank me for an easy final fight, but all credit where credit is due. Kitajima is a legend and is now a two-time World Champion.

Mong came over on the same trip to fight in the middleweight division. He'd retired from professional Muay Thai and had been training full-contact karate for about two years. This was only his second major tournament. The Japanese press and national TV station NHK were fascinated as to why a former professional five-time WBC World Champion and three-time Lumpinee Stadium Champion in Muay Thai would switch codes, coming all the way to Japan to compete in the Byakuren Karate World Championship. So, they did an interview and asked him a number of questions about his reasons for coming. In typical Mong fashion, his simple answer was, "I just like to fight and compete, no matter what the style."

The Japanese fighters didn't quite know how to handle Mong's fighting style. Being from Muay Thai, he had to concentrate a great deal not to punch to the head inadvertently. So, he didn't use his hands much, but his kicking style was unorthodox – always pushing forward and very aggressive. He kicked the karate fighters with full force, shin on shin, and with his shins seemingly made of steel, he left a number of them limping off the mat shaking their heads. He was the talk of the tournament, and in the end, became the Middleweight World Champion. What a freak of nature he is.

In the meantime, Anton seemed to be beating his cancer. But in 2009, his sister (after being declared cured) had a recurrence and they found the cancer had spread to her bowel and liver. I was very close to the Cavka family, and Anton's father, Dr. Anton Senior, used to refer to me as the fourth Cavka brother. So, when Jackie died in September 2009, I was as shattered as Anton was. I didn't know what to say to him. How can so much tragedy befall one family?

Yet again, Anton was there when I fought in the Byakuren Karate All Japan in November 2009, just like every other tournament. He must have really been hurting, and I wanted to win this one for 8him and Jackie. But it wasn't to be. Again, I got to the semi-final, and this time Kitajima knocked me out with one of his famous knee kicks. The funny thing is, I knew what his secret weapon was, and I was beating him on power and keeping my guard high to defend against such a kick. But I didn't even see it coming. Somehow, he launched himself from two meters away, and his knee came over my guard and clipped me on the chin. Third place again. This day was, without a doubt, one of my darkest hours. I'd come so close so many times, yet just missed standing in that coveted top spot on the podium. And I couldn't even do it for my best mate, who must have been so torn up inside but had still come to support me.

Some fighters say that winning a World Tournament is akin to winning the lottery. You can be the best fighter in the world and still not win. To win seven fights in one day, you must have some luck as well. I would prepare months in advance to make sure I was at my peak for these tournaments. I would then travel thousands of kilometers to Japan and arrive a couple of days before the tournament to give myself the chance to rest and acclimatize before the big day. It's not an easy thing to do, but it's common for all fighters who travel overseas to compete. The idea is to wake up feeling sharp on the day of the tournament and give it your best, fighting as good as – or better than – you did at your peak in the dojo at home.

To win on foreign soil, particularly, you have to beat each and every fighter convincingly, progressing through the rounds without collecting too many injuries along the way. You have to fight to the best of your ability, clearly dominate the local opponents with your power and technical ability, and never lose concentration. An *ippon* or *wazari* is the ultimate aim, but sometimes it can end up being a slugfest that goes to multiple extensions.

By the time you get to the final four, you are fighting superhumans. The elite of the elite, these guys are machines built in a different factory than the rest of us. They fight toe-to-toe and every punch and kick feels like a sledgehammer. Knockouts can come by losing concentration for even a microsecond. The top four fighters never take a backward step, show no pain whatsoever, and are as quick and dangerous as they are strong.

I was one of those top four fighters. Some would say I may have deserved to win, or that the judging was biased, or I was unlucky on that day. I'd say the better fighter won. I knew that we'd all trained as hard as we could, fought our hearts out, and left it all on the mat. Each and every time I came close to winning, I left determined to train harder and come back the tougher, more experienced, and better fighter. But by 2009 I was in my late 30s, running out of time.

Knocked out by Fathi in the dying seconds, I had come so close to winning. By 2009, I was wondering – particularly when I lost in the semi-final to the reigning World Champion, Kitajima – what the hell did I need to do to win that world title? I had come so close so many times, only to see it slip through my grasp. I was 38 years old, considered old for a tournament fighter, as most fighters peak in their 20s.

All three losses hurt the same. I can't really distinguish which was better or worse. They all hurt. Just losing concentration for a split second was the difference between me losing and a different champion being victorious.

I'll try to describe what this feels like to someone who doesn't do martial arts. The minute the decision goes against me, I'm emotionally devastated. I feel like I've let everyone down – including myself. Just five minutes before, I was strong and unbeatable, and then, in an instant, I was deflated, defeated, and powerless. It was even more frustrating because I knew I could have – or even should have – won, so to roll it all into one main emotion, it's just pure disappointment in myself.

I'd done weeks, months, and – if you consider that this was my whole life's aim – decades of training to get to this point. Of course, I never took anything away from the opposing fighter. My opponents deserved to be World Champions in their own right. They should be proud of that achievement forever. But deep down, I knew that it could have been different with any luck or twist of fate, with me lifting my hand as the champion. By this stage of my career, I was really beginning to think that this dream of one day being World Champion was going to be just that – only a dream.

Looking at us tournament karate fighters in front of thousands of spectators or on TV, it must look very glamorous. But let me describe the reality a little for you. There may be up to 128 fighters, and therefore we need to fight and win seven fights in one day against the best in the world to win the World Championship. So, we train our whole lives, day in and day out. If we are lucky, and win often enough, we get our airfares and accommodation paid to compete on the world stage.

We usually arrive about two days before the tournaments, landing on foreign soil with different food and a different climate.

We try our best to adjust, keeping our routines as normal as possible so that we'll be close to peak condition. But, it's almost a guarantee that on the day of the fights we will not be at 100 percent, or even as good as we were whilst training in our own country. At best, we hope to get as close to that condition as possible. Even at my best, that still means being at least 10% off peak. But on the day of the fights, the adrenaline often gets going, making up for the fatigue, time differences, foreign food, and lack of sleep.

The winner gets all the congratulations, the standing ovation from the crowd, gets celebrated at the afterparty, and remembered forever. But let me tell you the reality of the fighter who doesn't win, something with which I have a great deal of experience: imagine you go in with the expectation to win – which has always been my mindset. I've never entered a tournament just for the experience. I never saw the point of entering a tournament unless I thought I had a very good or better chance of winning. From my *uchi deshi* days onward every tournament I entered, I entered to win.

But now I was walking away from most tournaments with a trophy for second, third or fourth, absolutely gutted that I hadn't achieved what I truly believed I could. Of course, there were always people coming over to me and saying, "Well done," and "You'll get it next time," and I always appreciated their kind encouragement. I would attend the award ceremony in front of the crowd of spectators, a sayonara party if it happened in Japan, and then that lonely walk back to a small hotel room with my *dogi* and trophy in my bag. I would go back to my room and lie down to sleep, thinking about what could have been. It was the toughest feeling in the world, and by 2008 and 2009 I really started to question what I was doing with my life.

But, I was a graduate of the great Mas Oyama's three-year *uchi deshi* course, a Young Lion taught never to give up. So that was my resolve, and I would get right back into the gym and train even harder. I would never give up on my quest and one day, I would win. Or, I would die trying.

CHAPTER 14:
ARMY TRAINING AND SWAT

浪人

The Colonel's shadowy persona only grew larger the longer I worked for him. I've told you a little about his history in Thailand, but his 20 years before moving to Thailand are even more mysterious. If you're ever interested in reading about it, you can find it in his book, *Adapt and Overcome*. However, for all his wild tales, exaggerations, and sometimes-unbelievable adaptions of his past, there really is an incredible story to be told. If I were to compare him to someone else, it would be Robert Duval as Colonel Kilroy in the film *Apocalypse Now* - totally out of his mind but pumped for life like no other.

As a respected martial artist and trainer of champions in Thailand for so many years, at some stage he found himself ingratiated with powerful people. In fact, he was connected with high-ranking Thai officials and military personnel, and even a couple of Generals. His main business partner in his property development venture was General Pracha Promonok, one of the top-five military leaders who basically ran Thailand. This would surely be a great advantage in expediting their building projects, and no doubt a mutually beneficial relationship.

One of The Colonel's roles as a martial arts instructor was to regularly train the Royal Thai Military Police in Bangkok. He would train the regular military police in self-defense and hand-to-hand combat in a huge open-air shed on their military base. But at other times, he trained the Thai Special Forces at that same base. Anton told me that his idea for the documentary, *Journey to the 100 Man Fight*, came to him when he was watching us training 40 soldiers there. (Yes, I got involved with training Thai Special Forces and SWAT, as you'll read below!)

The soldiers were going through Hell Month in late 2008, the rigorous process of being promoted from regular military to military police. Typically, about 80 applicants began this course, but within a month of torturous mental and physical testing, that would be whittled down to only about ten inductees.

Anton came over in October 2008, finished with his chemotherapy but still very ill from its effects. He had helped The Colonel a great deal with translating and disseminating documents for the WKO in Japan through his company. So, The Colonel– as a kind of thank-you – asked him if he'd like to join us as an observer during training. I remember Anton asked The Colonel, "What do I tell the army people my role is?"

Without a pause, The Colonel handed him a Canon 7D camera and said, "Mate, you are the official photographer of the two-day training event."

Army Training And Swat

To The Colonel and me, this training was just a regular part of our job. But for Anton, watching us train the Thai military police in hand-to-hand combat, close quarter weapons training, and even sitting with Thai generals as they told war stories at lunchtime inspired him to eventually change his life's path to documentary filmmaking.

You may be wondering how the military whittled down 80 eager applicants - who were already special in their own right - to just ten by the end of the month? Consider that these soldiers were running ten kilometers every morning, ten kilometers at lunch, and ten kilometers each evening on top of a double session of other physically demanding activities, and you get the idea. It was a war of attrition, and even an injury meant the end for that particular candidate. The Colonel and I came in about halfway through the program, our martial arts training adding another aspect to what they were doing but also some variation to break the monotony.

Through The Colonel's strategic relationship and role training the Thai military, he was awarded the official rank of Colonel in the Thai Army. This may sound like some crazy story told by a loony expat, but in this case, it's actually true! To many people, Thailand is a place of white sandy beaches and cocktails with umbrellas, but it certainly has a dark side. If you really know how the inner sanctum of the Thai hierarchy works, it can be both complex and bloody at times - with a good dose of the Wild West thrown in.

THE RONIN YEARS

In 2008, there was a lot of political turmoil going on in Thailand. It marked the height of political infighting between the Red Shirts, who represented Prime Minister Thaksin Shinawatra and the working class, against the Yellow Shirts, who represented the royalty and upper class. Thaksin was originally from a peasant farming family but had entered the world of business and become a very rich man. He owned a communications company that he eventually sold to the Singapore government for nearly $2 billion U.S. dollars. Although a controversial figure, I guess he never forgot his humble beginnings (or where his votes were coming from). Once elected, he was a champion of micro loans – small loans that the bank makes to the peasants of Thailand, giving them the opportunity to compete (even if only in a small way) with the ruling class. This seemed to threaten the upper classes, upsetting the whole balance and order of things for hundreds of years. Hence, a political struggle for power began between the Red and Yellow Shirts.

Before Thaksin came along, the peasant class had never even bothered to vote, so the Prime Minister always came from the ruling class – which supported the rich staying rich and the king leading the way. However, with Thaksin's new policies and working-class support, he was in power from 2001 to 2006.

So, the opportunity arose for what became Thailand's first anti-terrorist squad, led by a New Zealand national living in Pattaya – The Colonel. Since a number of the local Pattaya police trained on a regular basis at the WKO *Honbu*, there was always a police presence there, and a close relationship between The

Army Training And Swat

Colonel, the police, military, and its generals.

In February 2008, The Colonel told me that he had been approached by the Chief of Pattaya Police and asked to form and train a Thai version of SWAT, or an anti-terrorism unit. I never questioned The Colonel in those early days, I just accepted anything thrown my way. So, we started down the path of forming a highly trained paramilitary squad.

I remember one week we had over 100 police from the local precinct come to the new five-story school, all trying out to qualify for our special unit. To test them, The Colonel made them go through weapons drills, scenarios involving pressure tactics, and simulated hostage situations, as well as a grueling series of physical exercises to determine who were best candidates. Of these 100 applicants, he chose twelve to continue the training.

Almost immediately, The Colonel began building the SWAT headquarters behind the school in Pattaya Klang. The local government gave him a budget to build the barracks, and with the funds they also purchased weaponry, which included M16s, AK47s, shotguns, Berettas, Glocks, stun grenades, and fragmentation grenades. We were also supplied with other tactical equipment such as grappling hooks, ropes, abseiling equipment, bulletproof jackets, and full SWAT uniforms that included protective goggles, gloves, boots, and balaclavas. Lastly, SWAT got a budget for three big trucks to get around in, one of which was a big yellow Hummer that had "SWAT" in huge black lettering down both sides. Looking back, this was a crazy time, and I often shake my head in disbelief.

Training started with two to three-hour sessions at least three times a week and went on for about six months before the Chief of *Chonbu*ri Police formally inducted us as Thailand's official SWAT squad. You have to remember that, aside from The Colonel and myself, the SWAT were all police veterans, so none of them were starting from scratch. In fact, as they were chosen from over 100 applicants, they were the best of the *Chonbu*ri area's police, and the six months of training just fine-tuned their skills in order to deal with specific terrorist threats. Mind you, the training didn't stop with our official induction and badge-receiving ceremony. It continued at two-to-three training sessions a week for the entire life of the SWAT team, which was about three years.

Where do I start with the training? What first comes to mind was learning how to handle automatic weapons – both rifles and handguns – at the local police shooting range. We had mock houses and terrorists set up, and we went through drill after drill in shooting the wooden terrorists and saving the mock hostages. We also learned to abseil out of tall buildings frontward, backward, and sliding face-forward down buildings, sometimes crashing through open windows into the buildings to tackle the terrorists in our mock scenarios.

For me, life up until this stage had been purely the life of a *karateka*. People who watch action movies may think that hand-to-hand fighting and weaponry go together, but this just isn't the case. They involve a very specific set of skills – and very different training to attain those skills. I remember the first time I abseiled from a 10-story building and what a completely foreign and scary experience it was. It just doesn't seem right to walk backward off the top of a building, even if you are strapped to it with a pulley set-up.

After we had been inducted, I remember doing a demonstration at the Pattaya Town Hall in the main town, and we all abseiled off the top off the 10-story building at the same time, in full gear, masks, and automatic rifles. Our trucks were waiting below, and we had all the local news and TV stations there to cover this event, as well as hundreds of local spectators. We descended, jumped into the cars, and sped off to action. The crowd clapped and cheered, and the chief of police looked very proud.

I remember seeing this event replayed later on the Pattaya evening news, watching myself masked up in a balaclava and protective goggles. Knowing that that was me, I laughed and thought about what sort of twists and turns my life had taken. I've learned time and time again that in life, the truth is without a doubt stranger than fiction.

CHAPTER 15: THE GOLD HEIST

浪人

"The most significant life is the one lived on the basis of a personal sense of justice and the desire to see justice realized everywhere."

–Mas Oyama

In May 2009, a group of renegade Cambodian soldiers came across the border into Thailand. They were armed to the teeth, on a mission to rob a series of banks and jewelry stores, then skip back into Cambodia once their newfound fortune was secured. I can't imagine that pay in the Cambodian Army would be great, so from a financial perspective, it probably seemed like a logical - albeit dangerous - way to go about getting their version of a retirement package.

Anyway, these guys weren't mucking around. There was six of them in a couple of cars filled with M16s and M18 Claymore mines, weapons I hadn't heard being used since the Vietnam War.

On May 15, 2009, the Cambodian rebels took on their first target – which just so happened to be a large gold and jewelry outlet in Jomtien, on the outskirts of Pattaya. It also happens to be where I was living and training with The Colonel and the newly formed Thai SWAT team.

The Cambodian rebels ran into a retail store in broad daylight, wearing army fatigues minus any insignias, balaclavas covering their faces, and brandishing automatic rifles. They proceeded to terrorize the staff and ransack the store of all the gold and jewelry they could carry before fleeing. An alarm was triggered, which alerted the local police. Within minutes, the Thai police arrived, guns drawn and ready for action.

Hearing the sirens from a distance, the rebels hopped into their two waiting cars and made their escape, racing off with the police in pursuit.

The police did catch up with them on the road, but the rebels started spraying automatic gunfire at the police cars and lobbing hand grenades out the window. One member of our SWAT team, Sam, was in pursuit; he copped a number fragments from one of the grenades, which bounced and then exploded on the road before bursting through the car door into his left leg. This caused the police to cease the chase, as they were clearly outgunned.

Coincidentally, Anton arrived that very night in Thailand. When he arrived at the karate school, he, The Colonel and I went to the hospital at around 11 p.m. to see how Sam was doing. The surgeons had already taken the fragments out of his leg, so he was recuperating in one of the private rooms along with his wife. The Colonel introduced Anton, and both he and I asked Sam how he was doing. He seemed in remarkably good spirits considering the circumstances. I remember The Colonel was concerned that there were no armed guards at the door, and Sam telling him he had sent them home. He said he could look after himself and pulled back his bed sheet to produce a silver automatic pistol while cracking a smile.

What was unknown to me then was that the Cambodian rebels, in their rush to escape, had left one of their own behind, who was captured by the police. The Colonel kept this from Anton and I but may have said something to Sam along the lines of, "Don't worry, we'll get them."

Anton went to his hotel, and I went home thinking all sorts of crazy thoughts. I knew we were training for exactly this type of situation, but I had never really considered that something like this would actually happen. At 12:30 p.m., I had been relaxing for about an hour in front of the TV when I got a call from The Colonel, telling me to be at the police station at 2:30 a.m. sharp ready for action. He didn't tell me how, but he said he knew where the rebels were holed up and that we were going in to get them.

We met at the Jomtien police station and suited up with all our gear, including automatic weapons, bulletproof vests, protective gear – the whole lot. The police station was a modern complex in the heart of town. We were given a briefing from the chief of police, Captain Napudon. The Colonel was absolutely pumped, and so were the other Thais. With one of our comrades having been seriously injured, and this being the first real test of our training, we were determined to make it 100 percent effective and accurate.

Off we drove into the night, the twelve of us in our three SWAT tank-like vehicles. I had no idea of the destination or distance, so I just sat quietly while we raced through the dark. It was a long drive, at least two hours before we got to our final destination. Five minutes before our arrival, one of the senior SWAT members got on the phone with what I found out later were the local police. They had also been notified of the Cambodians' safe house and were staking out the place from a distance. The police gave an update and a senior SWAT member relayed this information to the rest of us in the vehicle.

We arrived expecting guns blazing. Instead we found the local police surrounding a silent house. We leapt out of our vehicles just like we'd trained to do so many times before, taking up strategic sniper positions around the darkened house and waiting for orders. This was one of the most intense situations I can remember in my entire life. I was lying prone on the ground behind a bunch of bushes only meters from the house, waiting for orders on my walkie-talkie.

Would we open fire? Would they fire back? Or worse, throw grenades? Had they booby trapped around the house with Claymores that might blow us to bits the moment we tripped a wire, or just hit a remote detonator?

My body surged with adrenaline that was far different than any fight or tournament I'd been in. Just then, the front door opened and a plump, older Cambodian lady came out, yelling in broken Thai, "Please don't shoot! Please don't shoot!"

Our senior Thai SWAT member replied through the megaphone, "We know who you are, and we have the house surrounded. Come out with your shirts off and your hands in the air." I remember the old lady saying something to the effect of, "Please don't shoot my son. We will come out and do whatever you tell us to do."

She went back inside the house and within a minute, emerged with the remaining five rebels behind her, all with their hands held high and shirtless, as ordered. Immediately the head SWAT member yelled out, "Get on the ground with your hands behind your back," and half the team raced up to cuff them while the rest of us kept our guns trained.

The rebels were placed into two different police vans as we entered and secured the house. The array of weapons we found inside was staggering. These guys were career military and they had brought enough M16s, ammunition, and Claymore mines to start World War III. To this day, I wonder how things would have panned out if they had been alerted beforehand. Anyone who knows this type of weapon understands the sort of damage they can do. They are not toys; they are machinery of death, weapons of war. Claymores can remotely detonate and even be set directionally, firing hundreds of steel balls up to 50 meters with such force that they can incapacitate a whole squadron.

Our SWAT members jumped into the police vans along with

the handcuffed rebel soldiers and we headed back to Pattaya. The return two-hour drive was eerily silent. I was in a van with three of the rebels, who were cuffed and shackled. All of the SWAT still wore our balaclava so we couldn't be identified, and each prisoner had a ready SWAT guarding him on either side.

I remember that two of the Cambodian soldiers in my van looked as hard as nails. They had that killer's look, the so-called one-thousand-yard stare. I'd seen that look often with the veteran Thai soldiers I'd met in our trainings. But the younger Cambodian rebels didn't have that look yet. Before they'd killed anyone or seen death and destruction up close, they might have that wide-eyed look of naivety and adventure.

But now, something different was in their eyes: nascent panic, as they knew they were long past the point of no return. The prisoner I was guarding was just a young kid, no older than about 20, and he had this innocent, baby-faced look about him. Unlike his compatriots, his eyes were darting around and observing what was going on, terrified as to what was going to happen next. He glanced at me – and remember, I was wearing a balaclava – but my skin was white, unlike the other SWAT members, and I could tell from his expression that he recognized I wasn't Thai.

About an hour into the trip, we were handed bottles of water to give to each of the prisoners. Because he was handcuffed, the young kid couldn't open the bottle of water himself, so I did this for him and held the bottle to his lips from which he drank. After I gave him the drink, I remember he bowed slightly to me and

The Gold Heist

said *kob khun krap* or "thank you" in Thai. He just looked so young and innocent. I heard later that he was just the driver and took no part in the actual shooting, and during the trip I looked at him and felt extremely sorry for the situation he was in.

To be completely honest, I even fantasized about somehow opening one of the doors and throwing him out of the moving vehicle so he could get away and start his life again. Of course, I was never going to do this, but all I could think was that in the course of a couple of days, he had literally thrown his life away and sealed his fate forever.

This is Thailand, after all, and it doesn't take much imagination to consider what was going to happen to these guys at the end of the official investigation. There was no way that Thai society was going to pay to have these guys live the next 30 years in a Thai prison, yet alone for a proper trial. This happens to white westerners who do stupid things like smuggle drugs. The western press grabs these stories and the Thais are somewhat obligated to dole out justice similar to what might happen in the offender's home country. But these Cambodian soldiers, on the other hand, would never even be acknowledged by their own government.

They were deserters from their own army, committing crimes across the border against a government that they'd had disputes with for centuries. I hated to imagine their eventual fate, but at some stage it was likely going to be a bullet to the head in a dark field somewhere outside of Bangkok. And that's if they were lucky and it ended quickly, and not death under torturous conditions in some prison.

It was at this exact moment that I realized this wasn't for me. I was not cut out for this. I enjoyed the training but being a cop or solider was never me; it was not my nature. Capturing rebel soldiers might seem like an exciting life to some, but I didn't feel it was my role to take any part in doling out justice like this. I, myself, am far from a perfect human being, and if I were to be judged by a higher power, I can imagine being sentenced to a decent amount of time in purgatory myself! I decided that night that if someone was going to dish out justice to criminals, it sure as hell wasn't going to be me.

The next day was a complete circus. We brought the rebels to the scene of the crime and had them re-enact how it all panned out. The local TV stations and newspapers covered this, and we were feted as heroes. There are a couple of news clippings that I have kept from this incident, and I sometimes look back in amazement. It was a huge victory for The Colonel and the SWAT team, and I would have liked to participate in that celebration. But inside, I was in complete turmoil. I am a lifelong *karateka*. Being in the anti-terrorist police wasn't my calling.

Eventually, after about three years, the political situation calmed down and the SWAT team was disbanded. Although I learned a great deal from the training and had a great camaraderie with the other members, I was happy to be free of this burden and back to concentrating full-time on what I was born to do: teaching and training karate.

CHAPTER 16: TRAINING FOR THE 2010 WORLD CHAMPIONSHIP

浪
人

"If someone asked me what a human being ought to devote the maximum of his life to, I would answer: training. Train more than you sleep."

–Mas Oyama

Thailand proved to be everything I hoped it would be and more. After living there for only four years, I caught the eye of a beautiful and graceful Thai woman while I was on my lunch break from training at the gym. I'd seen her before, as we often ordered coffee from the same café. But this time, we gave each other a familiar glance and smile, so I said hi and started up a conversation. Luckily, she spoke basic English – about the same as I spoke Thai at the time.

She was beautiful and classy and polite, and I fell for her

straight away. Her name was Mothana Sriwattanapong, but she told me to just call her 'Mo' for short. We instantly hit it off. Coffee turned into conversations turned into long walks and meals out, and we soon started dating seriously. She was always so supportive and caring, and I adored her as much as I do to this very day. That's why I ended up marrying her!

With Mo in my life, I was even more focused on my goals. By this stage, I was 39 and, as I said before, running out of opportunities to claim a championship. The WKO was scheduled to hold their second biannual World Championship in October 2010, and I was going all-in. I'd let the last one slip through my fingers by getting knocked out in the final by the Iranian heavyweight champion, Amirhamzeh Fathi – I wasn't going to let this happen again. Like each loss before, I took that loss hard, and I tried to take my training to an even higher level to give myself a better chance of winning in the future. I always trained hard year-round, and at this stage, my training was a combination of martial arts, Army and SWAT training, weightlifting, and anything else that I thought would help. I was determined to leave no stone unturned, nor any potential reason for doubt the next time I fought.

Beginning about seven weeks out – which is about normal for fighters for these tournaments – I really stepped up my training. I started going all-out; no drinking or eating junk food and devoted myself to training at least twice a day, six days a week. Saturday was my recovery day, and Sunday was my heavy weight-training day to build core strength and power.

Training For The 2010 World Championship

Here is a look into my weekly training and nutrition schedule in the lead-up to a tournament. Unlike most people whose week starts on a Monday, mine started on a Sunday and looked like this:

Sunday: Wake up late, have a good sleep-in, order massive amounts of BBQ chicken and sticky rice around midday, and eat as much as possible for about one and a half hours. I picked up his tradition of nearly force-feeding in my old *uchi deshi* days.

I would have a bit of a nap until about 3:00 p.m., and then wake up and eat porridge for energy and carbohydrates. Finally, I would make my way down to the weight-training gym by about 5 p.m.

My weightlifting session was a solid two hours of concentrated explosive power exercises such as squats: three reps with 250 kilos; 180 kilos times 10 reps; up to 10 sets. I always considered squats the most important exercise, as kicking was my biggest weapon and legs were the most important instrument of destruction in full-contact karate. Legs are the foundation in all fighting.

Next were leg extensions and reverse curls for the same intervals. Then, heavy incline dumbbell presses, with short, sharp, explosive movements that I wanted to replicate my punches. I would do about four to six sets of 50 kilos on each side for up to eight reps.

Next was lateral pull-downs at ten reps and maximum weight, plus more added – really stacking on just about every weight in the gym that wasn't tied down.

Then there were variations of chins-up and dips with narrow and wide grip, and huge weights strapped to my belt – often 50 kilos or more. Occasionally, just for fun, my girlfriend Mo would jump on my back and I'd do as many dips as I could with her along for the ride! I would always try to rep out on the dip bar, and I remember doing 50, 60, and sometimes even 70 reps before failure. These were all incredibly good but simple exercises for core strength and power.

As I said, everything I did was fast and explosive – never slow – because in my mind I was trying to replicate punches and kicks and really get the fast-twitch fibers in my muscles going.

I'd walk out of the gym completely pumped and exhausted but thinking that it was a good session to start the week. To be honest, I really enjoyed the weights – and still do. Even though this was heavy lifting, and I always went to failure, compared to the intensive aerobic and torturous drills that awaited me the rest of the week, weights were the easy part of my schedule!

Monday through Friday at 9 a.m., I would wake for a slow jog to recover from weights the day before, covering about 5 kilometers. On alternate days when I didn't jog, I would begin with hill sprints. Then, the following day I used the rowing machine, then interval training on the stationary bike, and then Friday back to a slow jog again. This morning session was always an aerobic session, and I would mix it up with one day of torture (hill sprints, rowing machines, and the bike) and the following day with a relaxing jog, so as not to destroy myself and allow my body time to recover.

At 11 a.m. I would eat a massive bowl of porridge with a banana, some cinnamon for taste, and an avocado and four boiled eggs, eating only the egg whites.

At 12 p.m., I would go to work at the gym.

Lunch at 1 p.m. always consisted of huge amounts of rice, chicken or beef with vegetables, always loaded up with tons of garlic, for flavor but also to boost my immune system.

From 1:30 to 3 p.m. I would be at the gym meeting and greeting incoming students and patrons. This was my job as one of the main trainers and the face of the gym.

Next, 3 to 5 p.m. was boxing and Muay Thai training and conditioning class on the fifth floor. This involved at least ten rounds in the ring, five three-minute rounds on the heavy bag, and five three-minute rounds on the pads.

After that, I would get DT, Muay Thai legend Sak Mongkol, or any strong heavyweight who happened to be there to punch and kick into me as hard as they could while I stood there and took it. This was the key to my conditioning and preparation for what was in store in my tournament fight.

The first couple of weeks were the hardest because it was a huge shock to the system, but they were very important to set the foundation. So, I really suffered these first two weeks.

After all that training, at around 5 p.m., I started doing what I used to call "cranking it up." I would cross the road to the Carrefour Shopping Center and eat fried rice with chicken, and then crank it up with two cups of coffee, two jam donuts, a Snickers bar, and often wash it all down with an energy drink at the gym.

I needed to do this because a full day's training in the Thai heat would otherwise deplete my body of calories and zap all my energy. I would often weigh myself before the afternoon session at 3 p.m., registering about 92 kilos on the scale. By the time I reweighed myself after the evening martial arts class, I would usually come in at about 87 kilos. That's a five kilos loss in six hours – despite eating between sessions – and it meant I was losing liters of water during breaks in the classes.

In the early days, when I tried to eat clean with just rice, meat, and vegetables, I found I constantly felt flat. But as I got older, I learned that to be able to do these types of triple sessions in one day, I really had to crank things up in the later part of the day with pure sugar and caffeine.

The last and toughest part of the day was always The Colonel's torturous two-hour martial arts class. It was from 6:30 to 8:30 p.m., but it often blew out to 9 p.m. – and sometimes even later. This class consisted of a 30-minute warm-up, with all the usual push-ups, sit-ups, squats, etc., 30 minutes of kicking the pillars; and the last hour a combination of fighting drills, *Kumite,* and more conditioning. By the end, everyone who was in that class was alive in spirit only. Without a doubt, this is the sort of training required to produce champions. If you are not training this hard,

Training For The 2010 World Championship

you can be damn well sure that someone else who's training for the same World Championship is! So, if you want to win, you'd better be ready.

At 10 p.m., I would go back to clean eating, stopping in at a restaurant on the way home to get a fresh fruit shake, and then downing huge amounts of steak, vegetables, fish, and rice – you name it. To these waiters and waitresses, I was like a non-stop eating sideshow, and they'd giggle as they served my dishes.

Each day, I would also drink about five liters of water because I was sweating so much. I treated my nutrition and hydration as seriously as my training, and wrote down everything I ate, drank, and did each day. So, if one day I felt flat, I would look back through my diary and try to work out what I did right on the days I felt good, replicating that so I could continue to train as hard as humanly possible – and beyond.

I would taper off about ten days before the tournament and hope it was enough to win me a world title. All of that training was meant to condition my body to perform at my absolute peak on the day of the tournament, and I was 100 percent sure that I had trained at least as hard as even the toughest competitor there.

I would go into the tournament strong and confident, fight as hard as I could, and just leave it all on the mat, understanding that winners were made in preparation and training. Leading up to that 2010 World Championships, Mong was also training like a man on a mission, looking to avenge his loss at the 2008 Championships. To prepare for the tournament, Mong set a frenetic pace, running a half-marathon every day; 12 kilometers in the morning and 10 more in the afternoon.

He would also skip rope for five three-minute rounds, do five three-minute rounds on the Thai pads, and then we would work together, drilling different fighting combinations, before topping it all off with intense body conditioning. That was just a typical day

I remember seeing his face when he returned from his mid-afternoon 12 km run, covered in sweat and anguish. His face looked pained and distorted, like he had been to hell. But Mong loved to punish himself. Funny enough, he also loved listening to the Rocky soundtrack while he trained.

Every single day for seven weeks while training and preparing for the tournament, Mong listened to his favorite CD, the Rocky movie soundtrack. This was before high-tech blue tooth earbud headphones and such. So, when Mong put the Rocky CD in the gym's only stereo, it meant we ALL had to listened to the Rocky soundtrack on repeat! And we all knew not to touch the music player or risk the wrath of Mong.

Well, one time a newcomer to the gym decided he would change the music. He walked over and hit Stop and ejected Rocky and put on his own CD. Uh oh. To put it lightly, that did not please Mong at all. Mong stopped his training mid-kick, climbed out of the ring, walked over to the stereo, and smashed into the player with an almighty hammer fist.

The whole gym went silent and watched. He pulled the

Training For The 2010 World Championship

newcomer's CD out, threw it aside, grunted a few words and put his Rocky CD back in. I couldn't believe that the stereo was still working after that Mong hammer-smash, but on came the music from Rocky for the 1,458[th] time in a row!

No one said a word, and Mong climbed back into the ring and carried on training like a machine, happy once again!

CHAPTER 17: AT LAST

浪人

"No matter how strong the rival, the just will always win."

–Mas Oyama

I went into the 2010 WKO Championships the strongest and fittest I'd ever been. I wasn't nursing any injuries and felt like I was bursting out of my skin. But the competition, especially in the heavyweight division, would be especially fierce with some of the best fighters from around the world coming out for the title.

To become the 2010 World Champion, any of us would have to win six consecutive fights. My fights in the lead-up to the final went smoothly, and it seemed like I had the perfect preparation and execution. I was definitely not going to get knocked out this time; I was going to fight smart and keep my guard up at all times – something that had let me down before. As was often the case with the WKO World Tournament, there was a large contingent of Iranian, Japanese, and Brazilian fighters, and I'd say among the heavyweights, the Iranians were definitely the toughest.

In the first five fights, I scored a few early knockouts, which helped save me for the later rounds when I'd have to face the Iranians – which was always a war. I'd fought two of these guys two years earlier, so I knew I was in for a battle. But this time, I won by decision against both the Iranians I fought before the final. We stood toe-to-toe and literally smashed each other, not wanting to take a backward step, but my conditioning and strength prevailed. They may have been able to take the punishment for the first round and look like they were holding their own, but by the second round I found chinks in their armor and they began to falter. By the time it came to the last 30 seconds, I stepped it up, and in each case, I had them crumbling to the mat, clearly feeling the punishment. The judges awarded me the decision unanimously in both of these fights.

So, here I was at the final fight, probably my last chance at a world title – or maybe even the final fight of my career. Some of the guys I was fighting were half my age. My shins and feet were bashed and bruised from the previous two Iranian fighters, but I was still in the best condition I've ever been in going into a final. You wouldn't believe it, but the opponent I was facing Fathi, the very same 110-kilogram Iranian who knocked me out two years earlier with a rollover axe kick with only 30 seconds to go! But this time, I was all-too aware of his weapons and there was no way I was going to let that happen again!

From round one, we went straight to war, unwavering as

we slugged it out with the hardest punches and kicks we could muster. He tried his famous axe kick two or three times during the fight, but I had my right hand high and caught it each time. With a combination of fighting smart, moving around, picking my shots, and at some stages just throwing a flurry of sledgehammers, I felt I had the upper hand by the end of the first round.

The WKO rules call for an automatic two rounds of two minutes before the judges can make any decision – win, lose, or draw (in which case it goes another round). So, I went back to my corner when we got a 30-second break. In my corner were Anton, Glen, Mong, and Mutt. But for some reason, Nick Kara was on the other corner of the mat yelling out advice to me. I didn't think it odd at the time, but looking back, it was an incredibly smart thing to do. My corner was full of five voices all intermingling, whereas on the other side it was the Iranian guys yelling out to their countryman (which didn't distract me at all because I didn't understand Persian). Instead, all I could hear was Nick's clear and booming voice, which was a veteran strategy on Nick's part.

As I've said previously, Nick is a master tactician. After years of fighting and coaching, he's a genius at picking a fighter's strengths and faults and correcting them on the fly. I kept a clear ear to his advice and followed what he said to a T once the next round started. This time, it really paid off. I remember his instructions, including "Watch out for his left leg! Move to your right, Judd! Kick him inside the thigh!" as he could see my opponent getting hurt by my kicks and wanted me to take advantage.

To his credit and a testament to his strength, I can't say Fathi buckled from my blows, but I clearly controlled the fight and had more strength. When I heard Nick yell out "Last 30 seconds!" I gritted my teeth and went hell-for-leather nonstop.

Then, when I heard Nick yell, "Last 10 seconds!" I unleashed the most intense, furious series of nonstop punches and kicks probably in my entire career. It was going to all come down to the last few seconds but I was NOT going to lose this time. When the bag was thrown onto the mat to signal it was over and the referee yelled "*Yame!*", I knew I had won.

The decision was unanimous. Finally – after more than 20 years of fighting in tournaments – I was able to call myself World Champion. At the age of 39, I had prevailed and won the World Championship of the WKO.

This was the highest point of my tournament career. I had won the World Championship fighting the same guy who had beaten me two years earlier, which made the victory that much sweeter.

To this day, I will always thank Nick Kara for his advice, and my friends Anton and Glen for coming over and supporting me, not to forget Mutt and the rest of the WKO students. They really got me over the finish line. I can still hear Nick's instructions in my head, and they will never fade. Even in my sleep and dreams, I sometimes recall his voice in that final match. I'll happily fall asleep to that for the remainder of my days!

Anyone who has ever fought in the ring knows how

At Last

important the cornerman's advice is, and Nick got me through this last and most important fight of my life. I was now World Champion, and it felt like the weight of the world had been lifted off my shoulders. Adding to the joy was the fact that my training partner and compatriot, Mong, won the middleweight division. To be able to sit alongside such a fighting legend with both of us wearing our championship belts was an experience I'll never forget. I remember The Colonel being extremely proud, as he should have been his two best students had just taken on the world and won!

At the *sayonara* party, some of the biggest people in martial arts were present and offered their congratulations, which was a true honor. Ademir Da Costa, Kancho Sugihara, Kancho Mizuguchi, and Kancho Hasegawa were all there. To be feted by people I considered living legends, as well as branch chiefs from all around the world, was such a special experience. I finally felt that all my years of training had paid off, and that I had achieved my ultimate goal.

But strange as it may sound, it was just as important to me that night to head back to my apartment with some of my closest friends, including Anton, Glen, Mohammad, and Mehdei. I remember the power went out in my apartment, so we sat around by candlelight, sipping on beers until the early hours, talking about life and reliving what was my most golden experience.

I was 39 years old and had been fighting for over 20 years when I won the world title. The first world title I had fought in was the

World Open *Kyokushin* karate Championship in 1995, when I was only 24. Just like the Australian heavyweight title, which I won on my fourth attempt, after coming in second three times, I won a world title on my fifth attempt, taking two third place finishes and a second place before finally coming out victorious.

I had reached the pinnacle of my career, proving something to myself once and for all. But I finally saw it through Sosai's eyes, too - what he was thinking when he gave us countless lessons and words of encouragement throughout my many years of training.

If you have a dream and are prepared to train harder than anyone else, constantly learning and evolving in the process, anything is possible. No matter what obstacles get in your way, no matter how hard it seems at times or how long it takes, you need to remember just one thing: never, never, ever give up!

CHAPTER 18: UFC OR THE 100-MAN *KUMITE*

浪人

"The fastest way to attain courage is to follow the chosen Way and be willing to abandon life itself for the sake of justice."

–Mas Oyama

After winning the WKO World Heavyweight Championship, I felt as strong as I ever had. I actually felt that, even at this age, I was fitter, stronger, and faster than in my 20s. The victory instilled a new confidence in me, so I was looking for my next challenge. Since I'd joined the WKO, I had step-by-step increased my cross-training to all manner of martial arts. More than anything else, I wanted to gain an edge that would win me the World Championship. But in the process, I was also becoming quite an adept and skilled mixed martial artist.

In the beginning, it was cross training my *Kyokushin* karate with The Colonel's Kung fu. Of course, there was Muay Thai kickboxing and boxing on the fifth floor. I also became fascinated with the grappling side of martial arts and found myself training grappling every day in the afternoon with two Brazilian Jiu Jitsu guys, Paolo and Andreas Sinyorini. They really taught me the basics and piqued my interest in MMA and this new form of professional fighting called the UFC.

Not only that, but one of my good friends from Australia is five-time Olympic wrestler Cris Brown, who in later years would come over and train with us and bring some of his students with him. This increased my grappling and MMA skills exponentially. The idea of him bringing his students, such as the up-and-coming fighter Jordan Cameron, was for us to swap training techniques.

I remember one time when he brought Jordan over for a total of about three months to build up his stand-up fighting skills, which I had a great deal of experience with, of course, from my lifetime of karate fighting. In return, The Colonel often asked Cris to teach the class and concentrate on wrestling, so that would open up a whole new world for the WKO students. Cris is an extremely gifted wrestler, competing in the Olympics five times and ranking top-10 in the world for a total of 20 years, which is just incredible. He is a serious guy with a wry sense of humor and people idolize him in that world. Cris is perhaps the wrestling equivalent of Nick Kara when it comes to teaching ability. He, too, has an uncanny ability to wrestle someone while talking through the process of what he's doing, describing it to a tee. So, not only is he a legend in the sport of wrestling, but he's an incredible teacher.

Ufc Or The 100-Man Kumite

By late 2010, I was seriously considering fighting in MMA and, if successful, hopefully joining the UFC. Because I was cross-training with world-class fighters, I was able to gauge and test my skills with these fighters from a variety of martial arts. I found I could hold my own with some world champion kickboxers, Muay Thai fighters, of course karate fighters, which was my expertise. Soon, I could even compete with some very accomplished grapplers who came to the WKO to train. I still had a lot of fire in my belly at this stage.

It was late 2010 when The Colonel first approached me with the idea of the 100-man *Kumite*. 100-man *Kumite* is not something that someone just up and decides to do. It is an invitation-only event, almost always held in Japan, and the person who is invited is usually a recent All-Japan or World Champion. Not only that, but in Sosai's day, deep consideration was taken as to whether that person had the mental fortitude to get through such an inhospitable test.

In a tournament (which is no walk in the park itself!), you have to win seven fights against the best in the world, which adds up to perhaps two to four rounds per fighter. So, that's 14 to 28 rounds at the most over the course of the day. But the 100-man *Kumite* requires 100 one-and-a-half-minute rounds, against fresh opponents each time and without a break. It's a completely different – and, I can clearly say, insane – challenge, if you break it down.

The first time I heard about the 100-man *Kumite* was prior

to going to Japan, probably around the time I was going for my black belt at Shihan Eddie's dojo. It was a different era back then: no Internet, no way of confirming this type of unsubstantiated story unless you had the actual magazine article, photos, or could see it on TV. It was just a mythical story from Japan that was floating around the dojo among the students. I didn't give it too much thought, as I had more important things to concentrate on – such as getting my black belt and saving the money to get to Japan.

In 1988, I knew that Matsui was the World Champion, and I'd heard he had done this incredible challenge called the 100-man *Kumite* in 1986. But, at that time, I don't remember having seen any articles or write-ups on it. All I knew was that he was the best in the world, and I had my sights set on going over to train with him.

Mas Oyama originally devised the 100-man *Kumite* in the 1950s, legend has it to test his own capabilities and skills. But Oyama first decided to do a 300-man *Kumite*, with 100 fights each day over three successive days. He chose the strongest students in his dojo who were to fight him one at a time until they'd all had a turn. And then, they'd start from the beginning until the 300 rounds were up.

It is said that he defeated them all, never wavering in his resolve, despite the fact that he himself suffered severe physical injuries in the process. Each student had to face him about four times over the three days, though some never made it past the first day due to Oyama's powerful blows. Legend has it that Oyama even wanted to fight a fourth day, but no one else was willing or able.

Having set the example, Mas Oyama started to institute the 100-man *Kumite* as a requirement for attaining fourth or fifth *dan*. He soon found, however, that not everyone had the spirit to do it. Although physical skills could be taught, the indomitable will, courage, and determination – the "Spirit of *Osu*" in its extreme – just wasn't to be found in everyone. Thus, it became a voluntary exercise for those few who had the right stuff. Only a small number of people have ever completed the 100-man *Kumite* since Mas Oyama, a testament to just what an incredibly difficult challenge it really is.

The first time Sosai ever mentioned the 100-man *Kumite* to us uchi deshi that I remember was at one of the Saturday night dinners during my first year. He told a range of encouraging stories and one was the story of the 100-man *Kumite*. He explained this as the ultimate challenge, a physical and mental test of the human spirit for a *karateka*. He talked about the hardships and commitment to training that it would take, even just to have the slightest chance of getting through what seemed an almost impossible challenge.

Sosai's words were ringing in my ears about hardships he'd endured and battles he'd fought. He impressed upon us the lesson that through *Kyokushin* training, you could get through all of these hardships, to persevere and one day be victorious.

I guess, looking back, the 100-man *Kumite* was the ultimate test of not only the human spirit, but breaking through physical and mental impossibility to accomplish the inconceivable.

Sosai often talked to us young, eager *uchi deshi* about what it meant to be world champion, and also what it meant to be able to do the 100-man *Kumite*. He used to say that a great karate fighter should try to achieve two things in his life: to win the world championship and to complete the 100-man *Kumite*. I remember clearly that he placed the 100-man Kumite above winning the world championship. As students of Sosai Masutatsu Oyama, we *uchi deshi* were taught that finishing the 100-man *Kumite* was the pinnacle in martial arts, the ultimate achievement, and, in Sosai›s eyes, more glorious than even being a world champion.

My first live experience with a 100-man Kumite was in May 1991, when Akira Masuda was the last of Sosai's students to complete it while Sosai was still alive. I was a second-year *uchi deshi* at that time and the sacred event was held in the *Honbu dojo*. I fought Masuda twice, at number nine and number 67. In the first fight he was very strong, and in the second he was extremely fatigued and completely smashed up. He even started biting his opponents as he unearthed primal screams.

All the main karate branch chiefs came for this incredibly special and rare event. Less than a dozen people had ever completed it since Sosai first invented the challenge in 1950s. Those present included Sosai, second in charge of Shihan Goda, and all of his major advisors and branch chiefs. There were 50 opposing fighters, mostly black belts and a number of champion fighters, who had come from all over Japan to participate. Seated at the front official's table were Sosai, his ten officials, and Masuda's support team to the side. Shokei Matsui was very close to Masuda, giving cornerman advice but not participating as an opponent even though he was an instructor of the *Honbu* at the time. So, there were 50 fighters, 20 officials, 10 or 20 supporters of Masuda, 3 NHK cameramen, and about 10 members of the press. It was closed off to the public unless you were involved or inside Mas Oyama's inner circle.

You have to remember that the *Honbu* isn't as big as many expect for the world headquarters for such a huge organization. The floor space on the second floor is probably less than 80 square meters. On the day of Masuda's 100-man *Kumite*, Sosai got up first and gave a big speech about how special this event was and how only the very talented and mentally strong were ever invited to try.

Masuda's 100-man *Kumite*, of all those that were recorded, was one of the most memorable. He was battered like no other fighter I've ever seen. His fighting style, with hands jutting forward to block punches, meant that his forearms were torn up even before the halfway point. In the second half of the fight, he was in so much agony that he had shin guards not only on his legs but also on his smashed-up forearms so that he could continue. With members of the press and such an array of officials and fighters from all over Japan only added to the pressure he was under, as well as fighting under the watchful gaze of Sosai at the head of the table.

Masuda's 100-man *Kumite* was famous for its difficulty. But it's also been heralded because in the face of such incredible adversity he never gave up! He faced the toughest fighters in Japan at the time, and he was smashed time and time again. Eventually, he lost awareness of where he was, forgetting to punch and kick but screaming at his opponents as though his voice were a weapon, and even biting people. He showed a tremendous amount of spirit and inspired everyone in attendance, and later, those who heard about it.

He never gave up and never laid down, but was actually just a punching bag for the last 40 rounds, mounting little defense. But he never stopped! You could see in his eyes that he was absolutely exhausted, but something deep down inside of him pushed on.

Mas Oyama occasionally yelled out instructions and words of encouragement, also instructing the other fighters as to their duty as well. Near the end, at about fight 95 when Masuda was a complete mess and near collapse, Oyama stopped proceedings for a few seconds and said to the fighters, "Masuda is your *Senpai (senior)*, and you may feel sorry for him, but you have to ignore that. It is your duty to try to knock him down. You must block out the feelings that you have for him." He then pointed to Masuda, held up six fingers and said, "You have six more fights to go. Fight on!"

Masuda's last fight was with Mizuguchi, now a *Kancho* of his own breakaway group of *Kyokushin* and the same Mizuguchi who was present at my WKO win. He must have had some special relationship, friendship, or rivalry with Masuda, because the last fighter is always chosen because of some kind of personal history. Though nearly unconscious, fatigued and completely battered, Masuda completed his 100th fight.

In late 2010 (I can't remember exactly when) The Colonel approached the idea of the 100-man *Kumite* with me. His logic was sound. At 39 years old, if I decided to pursue professional MMA fights next, how many fights did I really have left in me? I was very confident of my ability to do well, but in his thinking, I might have only four to five fights at the maximum before age started taking its toll.

And usually, it would take at least this number of fights, if not more, to get the attention of the UFC before I could even join their ranks, and then perhaps the same number of fights again before I might start fighting anyone of world-class standards. That's assuming I would be successful, and not be injured through the initial induction.

But when The Colonel asked me if I would like to attempt the 100-man *Kumite*, my first reaction was a clear and concise "No way!" The reason for my initial refusal was twofold. I was a direct witness to the mental and physical toll Masuda's Kumite had in 1991. He spent a month in hospital recuperating from his injuries. Having witnessed this, you can only imagine my mindset in the face of my own invitation to do the same almost exactly 20 years later.

My second reason was the fact that as a fighter, as you get older, your ability to fight over a large number of rounds gets harder and harder. And I felt that the UFC or MMA, which only have three to five five-minute rounds, was something I was still capable of at this age. And, with my world-class explosive power, it was something I believed I could still do and be successful.

However, thinking about having to fight for over 100 rounds without a break against fresh opponents over three and a half hours just didn't make any sense. More importantly, at the time, this wasn't the direction I wanted to go. It just seemed too hard. It was an impossible task. I even said, "Colonel, I have seen this event and even participated as an opponent, and I know how hard it really is. There's a reason less than 20 people have ever completed it in almost 60 years."

The Colonel persisted, however, and repeated what he'd said before about my limited lifespan in MMA, and his confidence in my ability to do the *Kumite*. The Japanese elders had put out feelers to see if I would accept an invitation, and The Colonel kept saying, "Judd, you are the strongest fighter I've ever trained, you are the fittest you've ever been, and I really believe you can do this." And I did start thinking that *if* I could get through it at age 40, I would almost certainly be Sosai's last student to ever do so. Considering Masuda's near-death experience, was it even possible?

Those thoughts diminished as the year came to a close and The Colonel backed off somewhat. We had our yearly holiday break, and the idea faded.

As 2010 came to a close, I took a break over Christmas and the New Year. I was very happy about the fact that I'd achieved my ultimate aim in martial arts. I enjoyed being world champion, and I was able to relax, not having to think about what I was going to do next. At this stage, The Colonel's talk of the *Kumite* was something I just dismissed and put to the back of my mind.

But coming back to training in 2011, as the weeks and months went by, The Colonel brought up this idea of the 100-man *Kumite* again and again. Apparently, he'd discussed it with the heads of the WKO, and they agreed to extend me an invitation should I wish to take up the challenge. That's how the system has always worked, albeit usually strictly in *Kyokushin* circles. But, as you know, politics had torn me away from *Kyokushin*. A 100-man *Kumite* only happens about once every three to five years, and karate elders will only invite someone they think has a reasonable chance of success. But the invitation always begins as a sounding out of the fighter and his teacher, who can discuss and consider it. But only when the fighter commits will the formal invitation be extended.

However, I still wasn't giving it serious credence. I mentioned it to my best mate, Anton, over the phone and told him about the possibility of an invitation. He offered encouraging words, asking why I wouldn't at least consider it. I remember telling him, "Mate, you don't understand how hard this is." I shared my experience with Masuda, who almost died trying to do this 20 years earlier, and he agreed with me that it was something he knew nothing about.

But he did make the point that he'd seen me take my training to a whole new level in the past couple of years. Anton said I was the strongest, fittest, and most powerful he'd ever seen me, and he thought that if anyone could do the 100-man *Kumite,* it would be me.

Anton was scheduled to come over to Thailand with some friends for a training mission in March. Shane and Paul from my Chevron bar days, and Kieren, who was training up for an MMA fight, were coming along, too. About that time, The Colonel started asking me again about the 100-man *Kumite,* and my friends became part of the conversation. They, too, expressed their belief that if anyone could get through this, it was me.

Just their words of encouragement started me thinking about it. Perhaps it *was* possible? Perhaps I *could* do it? My best friend Anton coming to see me, after having beaten a very serious bout of cancer in the previous two years, made me think deeply about what I should do next. If he was able to get through such a terrible, tough time, and had such belief in me, then I wanted to live up to that. Anton's dad always showed me great respect, too, and I felt his family's hardship in losing their daughter and Anton's sister, Jackie, deeply. So, in some way, by accepting the 100-man *Kumite* challenge, I perhaps could return the act of faith that Anton had in me, while also giving Anton, his family, and all of my family and friends some inspiration for their own lives.

It's difficult to put into words my exact feelings and motivation at the time, but this is the best I can do.

In fighting in the world tournaments, it was more personal. It was more about me. Yes, I was representing my teachers and school, but it was my own goal. But the 100-man *Kumite* was something unique. This was on a completely different level, and my mindset and outlook were also changed. This time, I really wanted to represent my friends and family.

After about a month of training, Anton returned to Australia, but we continued the conversation over the phone. He even told me that he'd discussed with the Australian media the idea of documenting my training and the lead-up to the *Kumite*, should I decide to take up the invitation. I guess you could say by the time the boys left in late April, I had started to seriously consider the idea. Maybe I *was* capable of doing the impossible?! Maybe I *could* become one of those few supermen to get through this insane challenge. It was also a way of fulfilling my old master›s dream and honoring his memory. Please bear in mind that I was 40 years old by then, and those who completed 100-man *Kumites* were many years younger. Was it even possible, at my age, to take on what many karate elders call the ultimate test of the spirit?

By the end of April, and a number of phone calls later, I decided to say yes to The Colonel, the karate elders in Japan, and the WKO. So, in May 2011, I was invited by the WKO to attempt the 100-man *Kumite* in Osaka, Japan.

The wheels were set in motion. There was an official invitation sent out in Japanese on a scroll, inviting me to do the 100-man *Kumite* at the Osaka Prefectural Stadium. I remember a formal ceremony that took place in the WKO *Honbu,* in front of all the students, whereby I accepted the invitation from The Colonel. The date was set for October 22, 2011. Posters went up around central Osaka, and an announcement with a picture of me was placed in *Full Contact* magazine, saying:

The last *uchi deshi* of Sosai Masutatsu Oyama JUDD REID to do the 100-MAN KUMITE!

2011.10.22 SAT

Thailand Pattaya W.K.O. (World Kumite Organization) So-*Honbu* Shorin Kempo Shihan.

Osaka Prefectural Gymnasium.

There was no turning back now, and just attempting this Herculean challenge would take more strength, willpower, and belief than I could even imagine.

Sosai Oyama training in the Honbu Dojo, Japan, 1990.

The 1993 uchi deshi class with Sosai Oyama.

Sosai Oyama at Honbu Dojo, Japan.

Judd's uchi deshi graduation day, March 1993.

THE RONIN YEARS

Judd on the banks of the Yarra River in Melbourne, Australia.

Judd's 2nd Dan grading, 1991.

Anton and Judd out and about in Tokyo in 1995.

Judd, Joe Sayah, and Scott Powell working at the Gas Panic Tokyo night club, 1995.

1995 World Tournament in Japan. From left to right: Mike, Kayo, Nick Zav, Adrian, Murf, Duncan, Joe, Maho (Anton's girlfriend), and Anton.

At the 2010 WKO World Tournament: Sugihara Kancho, Mong, The Colonel, and Judd. Both Judd and Mong took home championships from that WKO tournament!

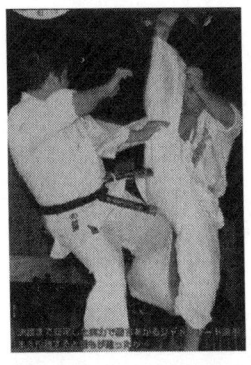

Judd with an axe kick at the WKO World Tournament in 2008.

Mohammad (Double Tap) and Judd - training partners and great mates!

An article on Judd in Australia's Penthouse Magazine. To this day, I have no idea how this story ended up in the magazine!

THE RONIN YEARS

Judd and Nick Kara at WKO - training partners and lifelong friends!

Judd training with the anti-terrorism unit, SWAT.

At the back of the WKO and SWAT headquarters.

Fight number 60 during the 100-man kumite in 2011.

At the 100-man kumite with the best friends and the best support team, Ned, Anton, Paul and Nick.

Judd and The Colonel.

Log training in the Dojo. One of devices used in preparation for the 100-man fight and tournaments.

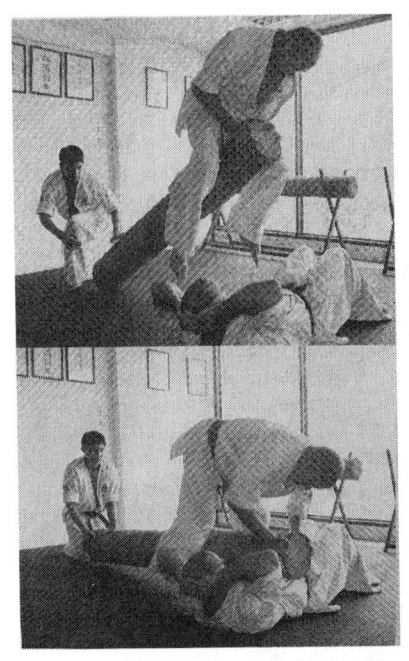

Body conditioning using the log. The Colonel showing no mercy, getting Judd ready for the 100-man fight.

Afternoon training on the top floor of the Honbu Dojo in Thailand.

THE RONIN YEARS

Judd, Mo, and Anton kicking it at Anglesea in Melbourne, Australia.

Screening of the 100-Man Fight documentary at the Astor theatre in Melbourne, Australia.

Anton and Judd at the Arnold Classic in Melbourne, Australia - looking very cheeky!

Anton and Judd in Cambodia working on The Young Loins book.

Anton and Judd kicking back in the pool overlooking the Mekong River in Phnom Penh, Cambodia.

Anton and Norm ride in a tuk tuk in Phnom Penh, Cambodia (Judd took the photo).

Los Angeles, California seminar with Tom Callahan, Dolph Lundgren, and Judd.

Judd visiting the apartment where he lived for one year in 1982 at Earls Court, London.

The Young Lions book is published in 2016.

Brooklyn, New York seminar.

THE RONIN YEARS

Training camp in Bangalore, India.

Visiting the pearl of the world, The Acropolis in Athens, Greece.

Brooklyn, New York seminar.

Australia vs Japan tournament in Melbourne, Australia.

London seminar.

2018 Uchi deshi Thailand camp.

Dean and Judd as the sun goes down on another successful uchi deshi Thailand camp.

Dean, Norm, and Judd at the uchi deshi Thailand camp.

THE RONIN YEARS

Quan and Nathan after running the dreaded "Hill of Death" at the uchi deshi Thailand camp.

Beach training, uchi deshi Thailand camp.

Judd's weekend camp in Costa Rica. *Pura Vida*, as they say!

Uchi deshi Thailand camp.

Little Max sitting in Seiza at the first uchi deshi camp in Thailand.

Friday night class at the Chikara Dojo.

The Chikara Dojo.

Chikara Dojo, Melbourne, Australia.

THE RONIN YEARS

Mo, Max, and Judd at one of the Chikara tournaments.

Chikara students receiving their certificates after passing belt grading tests.

A happy family at the reception area of Chikara Dojo.

CHAPTER 19: KING OF TOKYO

浪人

"Reading good books implants good ideas in the mind, develops good aspirations, and leads to the cultivation of good friends."

–Mas Oyama

When I accepted the invitation to the 100-man *Kumite*, Anton began pitching the idea of doing a story on the event to local Australian news programs such as *60 Minutes, Australian Story*, and *Sunday Night*. As I've said before, Anton is a guy who believes anything is possible. He'd gone from nothing – a foreigner with no money, no contacts, who didn't know the language, and had no idea about Japanese business culture - to becoming the King of Tokyo in just a decade and a half. But after almost dying from cancer and losing his sister around the same time, he retired from the car business and returned to be with his family in Australia.

Anton shared with me the first time he got the idea to make a documentary about my life. It was when he came over to Thailand in October 2008 and was watching The Colonel and me train the Thai Special Forces. We had completed two days of training, and one of the Generals, The Colonel, Anton, and I did some target practice with handguns. By that point, doing this sort of thing on a military base had become quite normal to me, but Anton was astounded.

He told me later that this was his first inspiration to make a film about me, and the 100-man *Kumite* would be the ideal storyline to tie it all in. He felt I didn't have the worldwide recognition I deserved outside of karate circles, and his documentary, titled *100 Man Fight,* would put the life of a full-time *karateka* in the spotlight.

"No problem for me," I thought. If I was doing the 100-man *Kumite* anyway, we might as well record it, so I could watch it when I got older or share it with students. Little did I know what a hit this humble film would become in martial arts circles once it was all done.

Anton and I had been friends for over 20 years by that point, so I also knew to trust his instincts and his intelligence. I was about 16 or 17 years old when we met. My old school friend, Nick Murphy, said one day, "You should start doing weights to prepare for Japan." Nick mentioned that he trained with this guy named Anton Cavka, and I'd get a lot out of his training. So, that's how I first met my crazy mate, Anton.

I went to see Anton at this small but serious weight-training space called Moonee Ponds Gym, popular with Melbourne's security pros and tough guys. Nick introduced me to Anton at the gym. My first impression was, "*Jesus, who is this beast of a teenager?*" He was about a year and a half older than me but wasn't built like an ordinary teenager. He wasn't that tall, only about 5'10", but weighed about 95 kilos of packed muscle. Actually, it was just a quick introduction before we got straight into the weights. Anton didn't talk much that first day. He was just there to smash the weights.

This was a hardcore gym. Anton led the way and skinny me tried to keep up, but I was only half his strength. Anton took no breaks. I thought it would be a casual workout and "nice to meet you, buddy," and we'd plod along, but there was no chance of that. Anton was on a mission to do every exercise and wreck himself – and poor old Nick and me, too. Later on, I felt privileged to train with him because there was no mucking around. He could arm curl two plates, which is 100 kilos, and squat three plates easily. I wonder what the older guys in the gym thought of us young kids? For sure they must have respected Anton, as he was going as hard as he possibly could. How could they not think, "Good on you, kid!"?

"*He's no kid, he's an animal!*" I thought as we trained. Terminator is a more appropriate word for Anton. He really was my inspiration. Even though he completely wrecked me every session, I was thankful for the chance to train with this crazy Terminator with blonde dreadlocks.

I pretty much only saw Anton in the gym in those early days until I was 19 and went to Japan. There was no doubt about it: Anton was wild, almost caveman wild, but very smart as well. His mates were pretty crazy, too, but all good guys. They had a spark in their eyes and there were no limits, no boundaries, no rules. They were free in every sense of the word and doing what all teenagers should be doing: being happy and living life to the fullest.

I remember Anton and the crew taking me out for the first time, to a bar called Zu Zu. I had never drunk alcohol in my life, but they ordered me something called a Flaming Lamborghini. It was a mix of three different spirits, with the top set on fire for good measure! I had to use a straw to drink it down as quickly as possible before it melted.

I had one of those and I was gone, while Anton and the boys had three each and didn't even seem drunk. There were no half-measures with them. Good thing they were looking out for me. I really had a great time with Anton and the boys. They were on a mission to meet as many girls as possible, calling all the girls "sweets." Especially Mike, Anton's younger brother, who looked like Jim Morrison from The Doors. They were carefree guys, crazy but harmless (well, maybe only to themselves), but not troublemakers at all.

Anton was the strongest and took care of the pack. He'd be the first to jump in if there was any altercation and Melbourne was a rough place in those days, so he had plenty of street fights.

King Of Tokyo

By the time I went to Japan, Anton and I were good mates, so we kept in touch as much as possible while I was overseas in the *uchi deshi* program. Four years later, I returned to Oz and caught up with Anton. We all had grown a lot and changed, as young people do, but even more so because of our intense training.

That's when Anton's Japanese odyssey all started - from that one round of golf we played together. I was talking about my life in Japan and said I'd be heading back there soon. Over nine holes, I talked Anton into coming back with me. He had finished university with an economics degree and was such a clever guy, but not much was happening in Oz at that moment. So, he agreed to come to Japan and teach English.

I remember Anton's early days in Japan fondly. At this time, we were all living in a *gaijin* house with Joe. One day, Anton went for an interview for a job as a ski instructor at one of the ski resorts in Japan. He was all pumped about getting this job

Not wanting to be left out, I said, "What about me? I want to be a ski instructor, too!"

Anton asked, "Can you ski?"

I said, "No, but I lived in Sweden for six months. That's good enough."

I kid you not: I immediately rang up the manager of the resort and spoke to him in Japanese. The guy asked, "What level skier are you, level A or B?" Not sure what to answer, I said, "B grade," and he answered, *"Ah sugoi na!"* which means "very good."

THE RONIN YEARS

He offered me the job right there and then!

The problem was, I couldn't ski! I literally had never been on the slopes or skied before in my life.

So, I ended up calling up the next day and canceling the ski job. What were Anton and I thinking? Since then, I've seen Anton ski. Yeah, he's okay, but it would have been a *Dumb and Dumber* moment with the two of us on the slopes. It just shows how eager we were to give anything a go!

Instead of a career as a ski instructor, Anton worked hard as an English teacher for about four years, continuing in Japan after I went back to Oz. We became best mates while we lived in Japan, even though we didn't talk for a whole month at one stage because I ate a piece of his chocolate cake from the fridge. To be fair, I thought he didn't want it. We were both stubborn, but at the end of the day, we had each other's backs.

I returned to Oz about ten years ago, but Anton ended up staying 16 years in Japan. Now remember I said he was clever; he was also extremely motivated, a great combination. His company, Japan Auto Direct, ended up being one of the most successful car export businesses in the entire country.

You know all those Japanese imports you see on the road, the ones straight out of the *Fast and Furious* movies? There's a good chance they came from Anton. The guy was a machine, typically working 16-20 hours per day. We would chat often and catch up in Thailand now and then. I had to take my hat off; nothing was too hard for him. If he put his mind to it, it was going to get done.

King Of Tokyo

Each time I visited him there, he was dating a new supermodel and driving the latest Skyline, Hummer or Mercedes. I started calling him the King of Tokyo.

Anton became my closest mate. I love him like a brother, so he has been known by many nicknames over the years, including: Tonnsa, Tones, Soldier, Bear, and now, the one that suits him the best, which I gave him: The Mechanic! It's from an old Charlie Bronson movie, and a remake was done by Jason Statham recently. I call him this because no matter what the task or how difficult it is, he will find a way and get it done. Perhaps it's his obsessive-compulsive behavior, but Anton is just driven in a special way, pouring his heart into any project that he undertakes.

Anton always treats everybody with respect, and although he might get on peoples' nerves sometimes, it's only because he's so intense. This is why he will always succeed. I'm very proud to call him my friend, and people always say, "Judd, you've got Anton on your side, and he's a hell of a bloke. With him looking out for you, you guys are always going to do great."

The biggest thing is that Anton isn't scared of a damn thing in this world. He has no fear. He will attack any challenge head on, but with intelligence. We have a favorite saying, "Charlie don't surf," taken from the Francis Ford Coppola film *Apocalypse Now*. To us, this means we can do anything we put our minds to. Never give up.

With all this in mind, imagine you've spent the last decade

selling cars around the world and then, one day, you decide you're going to make a documentary and film it in three different countries. This is just like the Anton I've always known. No hesitation. He just dreamt it up and did it.

He'd approached several Aussie TV current affairs programs with the concept, but they decided filming overseas would be too expensive. That rebuke just made Anton more determined. So, he decided to "guerrilla" film it himself. He just grabbed a couple of guys fresh out of film school and bought a couple of cameras to shoot everything himself.

In typical Anton fashion, he pulled it off magnificently!

Charlie, don't surf!

CHAPTER 20: FRIDAY NIGHT TRADITION

浪人

Professional fighters from all over the world frequently came to train at the WKO, and that included some colorful characters. I've already told you about Mong, The Colonel, the incredible Double Tap, Nick Kara, and WKO visitors like Cris Brown. But a couple of them were almost unbelievable, even for the crazy fight world.

We once had this Russian guy named Dennis train with us in Thailand for about three months. Well, maybe that wasn't his name, but he called himself Dennis for some strange reason. I think his real name was Boris or something like that, and he was a real nut. But I have to give it to the guy: he got hammered by everyone but kept coming back. Double Tap (Mohammad) and I would say to each other after he left, "Where is Dennis? We miss him?"

Not only did Dennis do the traditional martial arts classes at night, but he would also take Muay Thai, boxing, and MMA classes – any kind of training that he could do. Of course, that was admirable. But every night before class, he would come to the dojo early, put on his Walkman's headphones, and then tie a string around his head that was attached to a tennis ball. He would try to do exercises made famous by Russian/Australian boxer Kosta Tszyu, punching the tennis ball while it was attached to his head, attempting to time it perfectly as it sprung back on the string. Kosta Tszyu makes it look so easy, but Dennis was far from a Kosta Tszyu. He kept completely missing the ball, which would spring back and smack him in the face. Wap! Wap! This happened class after class and provided us with a lot of amusement, but Dennis never caught on because he always had his headphones on.

One day just before class started, I asked Dennis, "What kind of music are you listening to?" I was expecting a reply of perhaps the Rocky theme song (Mong's favorite), or something similar to pump himself up.

He offered his earpiece so I could listen, and I heard nothing but a Russian person speaking. I said, "What's this?"

Denis replied, "The Russian news."

I went and told DT and we both cracked up laughing. Dennis was a few cards short of a deck, that's for sure.

Of course, I respected anyone who put in a great effort, and Dennis was strong and could hold his own. But he often went too far, and the consequences were disastrous for him.

On the first occasion, Dennis was training with Cris Brown,

Friday Night Tradition

the Aussie Olympic wrestler, and was only supposed to grapple. Instead, Dennis started throwing wild blows at Cris' head.

"What the hell?" Cris yelled, and with one punch, pretty much knocked Dennis out. The next day Dennis came back with a massive black eye, which provided a good target for his tennis ball. Wap! Wap!

Dennis started to go hard with DT in the next sparring session, so DT double tapped him. Luckily for Dennis, he just kicked him in the guts and dropped him, not the head. A few days later, Dennis fought a friend of mine, Nigel, and slammed him onto his head, hurting him. Dennis was out of control and had to be stopped.

So, I jumped in the ring to fight him next. Straight away, Dennis charged at me like a bull and tried to take me down. So, I sprawled on top of him and stood quickly back up. Now my adrenaline was pumping, and it was time to stop this maniac. I unloaded with a low kick as hard as I could. He buckled, and then I unloaded again straight into the same thigh.

Poor Dennis was lying on the floor writhing in pain and literally rolled himself out of the ring. I felt a bit bad, but that's what had to be done in my eyes. I could have kicked him right in the head, but that would have been nasty. I jumped out of the ring and asked if he was okay. Of course, he wasn't. He was holding onto his leg and rolling from side to side.

The next day, guess who rocked up? Dennis, ready to train again! What a champion. So now he had this big black eye, probably broken ribs from DT, and was limping all over the place from my two thigh kicks. I had to take my hat off to the guy.

Perhaps a week later, Dennis wanted to spar with me again. Already, in my head, I decided I wasn't going to go hard on him but wanted to teach him the right way to train hard without hurting anyone.

But right before we squared off, Dennis said to me in broken English, "Please, Judd. Control! Control!" meaning, take it easy on me and control your fighting. I shook his hand, and said, "Of course, mate." So, we went at it very lightly.

From this day forward, if we noticed any newcomers with Dennis's traits or characteristics, DT and I would instantly say, "We have another 'Control' training here." We would both burst out laughing over that. "Control, Control. Wherever Denis is, I hope he is okay and listening to his Russian news. Wap! Wap!

That was life in the gym, and honestly it was amazing that so many adrenaline-fueled fighters from so many cultures and countries fit in with so few problems. We were all there for the same purpose: to train hard and push ourselves to be better. And that's what we did day in and day out with little variation.

Even Fridays, when others may slack off a little, was one of my biggest training days. First was the 1 p.m. SWAT training session, which usually involved various outdoor training drills. Thailand's heat is something else, and nearly 100 percent humidity made things really interesting when you were wearing army pants, a bulletproof vest, cap boots, carrying your side arm,

Friday Night Tradition

and an M16 strapped over your shoulder. Sweat would pour from us profusely, and even the Thais would be sweating like crazy, which is unusual for them.

One of the drills was to sprint to the top of the 6th floor, attach ourselves to a rope, and abseil down the face of the building, either forwards, backwards, or face down.

Even the smallest error while attaching yourself to the rope would mean certain death, or at least being in a wheelchair for the rest of your life. You need to have faith in your equipment and your drill sergeant. With The Colonel, however nuts he was, I had total faith in him and trusted his every word.

At the start of this abseiling, I was absolutely terrified and thought this was the end of me! But within a short time, I loved it and it was a huge adrenalin rush. We would reach that top floor, attach our carabiner to the rope and literally launch ourselves off the roof with the M16 pointed forward. We'd try to hit the ground smoothly, sprint towards a target, and sometimes break fall over a car which was set up just as an obstacle for us to get over. The Colonel had us on a timer and demanded 100 percent effort and perfection. He would yell out *lao lao*, which means "hurry up" in Thai and *Ao ik, Ao ik,* means one more, one more.

I have to admit that I started to really like this SWAT training. My heart raced; lactic acid surged throughout my body; the heat, fatigue, and sometimes dizziness was insane; but this is what I needed. I looked at it as extreme strength and conditioning training, building physical endurance as well as mental strength.

I was fired up and wanted to beat my fastest time. *Let's go, let go,* I muttered to myself, *lao lao!*

Another one of my favorite drills was running up to an open window of an apartment building and launching myself through it, break-falling on the other side. We practiced breakfalls as a warm-up in classes, but this was taking it to another level. I remember chuckling to myself and thinking that if things don't work out here in Thailand, I could always be a stunt man in the movie business!

Anyways, after an hour and a half in the blazing sun, our Friday SWAT training was done. I had about 30 minutes of rest before the 3:30 Muay Thai/kick boxing session, followed by the 7 p.m. advanced class. Nick Kara and Mohammad DT were awesome, always encouraging me and saying, "Go Juddo, you're taking your training to another level."

I always dragged my feet out of the dojo after those marathon Fridays. Reaching home after a massive feed, stomach full, barely able to stand, I would toss my bag over my shoulder and head up the stairs to my apartment on the 5th floor. Now what made this last bit of the Friday journey really interesting was that I took my M16 machine gun home with me.

Walking up those stairs with a sports bag and a machine gun over my shoulder must have been some sight. My apartment was totally visible from the street so people could easily see me. I was too tired to really think about it, and just looked at those bloody stairs as a nuisance and my last little challenge for the day.

Friday Night Tradition

Entering the apartment, I quickly ditched the bag on the ground and tossed the burner (M16) under the bed, mission done.

I loved my life in Thailand. Yes, I worked hard but I was doing exactly what I wanted to do. Nowadays, the conversation is all about pain, punishment, and sacrifice to reach your goals. But I never felt any of that in Thailand; it was just sunny beaches, palm trees, training, and happy days.

Friday was also my night to let my hair down and unwind since there was no training on Saturday. Anton was spending a lot of time in Thailand around this time, so I wanted to hang out with my mate and have a few drinks and some laughs. DT would join us on our Friday night tradition, as well as anyone else who was in town at the time. Russ, Nick Beggs, Scott Powell, and Donny would always head over to my joint if they were in town. I had a large TV and an awesome stereo system set up in the lounge room. We would kick back, drinking Sang Som (a strong but cheap Thai spirit) with Sprite and Red Bull. Anton was an *Apocalypse Now* fan and knew every word of it by heart.

The opening scene always set the mood: "Everyone gets everything he wants. I wanted a mission, and for my sins they gave me one. Brought it up to me like room service. It was a real choice mission and when it was over, I never wanted another."

About an hour into the movie and one bottle of Sang Som down, Red Bull coursing through his system, Anton was truly fired up.

"Run Charlie!" Anton would scream at the top of his lungs,

mimicking the scenes from the movie. He would grab the remote control and turn the volume up to the max. The scene where they are headed into the village with the composer Wagner playing from the speakers attached to their helicopter sounded awesome on the surround sound. Anton would yell it all out line-for-line with the American accent to match. He was hilarious - Francis Ford Coppola would have loved Anton and given him a part in the movie, for sure.

After two hours of drinking, he fast forwarded to his favorite scenes, perfectly in character with whoever was on the screen. Anton was mostly in charge of the remote, so Russ, Beggs, and the boys would pour the drinks and keep the show rolling. Another favorite movie was Quentin Tarantino's, *True Romance* and Mel Gibson's movie *Apocalypto*. They were all action-packed movies, with a story to tell and a mission to be completed.

We were all on a mission in Thailand, as well, and the comradery and support I got from my friends meant a lot to me. I truly don't think I could have made it through all of the intense training without them, and I always missed my Aussie mates when they weren't around for our Friday night tradition.

Eight weeks out from a tournament, our Friday night traditions and my surround sound would have to be put on hold. I'm sure my neighbors were pretty happy about that as well.

On one particular Saturday after our Friday night tradition, we had to get up early to go to Bangkok for some army training. The Colonel allowed Anton and his crew to come along to film

Friday Night Tradition

and we thought it would be a great addition to the documentary. However, the film crew did not pull up okay from our previous big night. Both Anton and I were a little hazy as well and had to put on our best poker faces just to get through the day. Ben, the cameraman, was a literal mess. His scruffy appearance was something out of *The Hangover* movie, in fact, at the end of this day, his new nickname would be Hangover.

The Colonel pointed out that the light on Ben's camera wasn't on, so for the first 30 minutes nothing was recorded. The Colonel even laughed and said, "You had a big night last night, hey." After the first session, we all went for lunch. At the lunch table, Ben asked where the toilet was. They gave him some simple instructions and off he went. About twenty minutes later and at the end of lunch, Ben still hadn't returned. The Thai Colonel called one of his soldiers to go and find Ben.

Within a few minutes, he returned with Ben. The soldier said he found him passed out in the bushes. The Thai Colonels all cracked up laughing and The Colonel just shook his head. But they were super cool about the whole thing. Ben said he couldn't remember what happened and felt dehydrated and dizzy. It was boiling hot in that training area, but Ben was doing the best he could in that situation. So, with the little nap in the bushes and the water and packet of electrolytes we gave him, he was alright to continue.

But Ben's hangover nightmare was about to go from bad to worse. At one point, The Colonel was demonstrating how to do one arm push-ups. Hangover Ben must have got a surge of confidence (or delusion) after his nap in the bushes and remarked to The Colonel that one arm push-ups weren't that hard. Uh oh.

We all started laughing at Ben because he looked in no shape to even do one push up. The Colonel immediately challenged Ben, "If you can do 10 push-ups, I'll give you 1,000 dollars. But if you don't, we will shave your head."

"No worries at all," said Ben, ever-so confident (or still drunk). With all of us watching in amusement, Ben attempted a one-arm push-up and fell straight on his face. We all broke out in hysterics. As Ben peeled himself up off the floor, the Thai soldiers ran towards him to grab him. Ben tried to run away, but to no avail. They dragged him back and sat him down and proceeded to shave his head.

We even got this all on film and added it to the documentary. You can even see Anton mentioning that the army barracks was a serious place surrounded by high walls and soldiers, and then there was Hangover Ben putting on a one-man comedy show. Unfortunately, we didn't film the bit of him passing out in the bushes!

There were numerous funny occasions during the filming of the documentary, as well as at the gym from day to day. I appreciated the change to get to know all of these guys, from film crew to Thai soldiers to other fighters, and looking back, those light-hearted memories together are the ones I really cherish.

CHAPTER 21:
TRAINING FOR THE *100-MAN FIGHT*

浪人

"Subjecting yourself to vigorous training is more for the sake of forging a resolute spirit that can vanquish the self than it is for developing a strong body."

~Mas Oyama

My preparation for the 100-man *Kumite* was going to be completely different from any training I'd done before. Over the years, I'd devised a system for training for tournaments that consisted of months of strength and conditioning exercises, cross training, and learning new techniques in the off season, all culminating six to eight weeks out from the fight. Then, I would ramp up my super-intensive cardio training, sparring and conditioning in the lead up to fight day, hoping it would all take me to an even higher level. The goal was not just to enter a tournament or even do well, but to win it – every single time.

But the 100-man *Kumite* presented a totally different

challenge, one that was almost impossible to plan for since this *Kumite* was an incredibly rare undertaking. When I was training for the *Kumite,* there were only 17 others who had completed it as far as I knew. And the ranks of those who had even witnessed a 100-man *Kumite* were limited to perhaps to a thousand people in the entire world – if that.

So, when it came time for me to map out my training strategy there in Thailand, I was one of the few people on earth who even knew how something like this was going to go. It was all based on my one experience with the All-Japan champion, Masuda Akira, undertaking the 100-man *Kumite,* which didn't exactly inspire confidence.

I was 20 years old at that time, in my second year as *uchi deshi*, and fought Masada twice in his 100-man *Kumite.* The first fight was his ninth when he was still incredibly strong and fresh, and he nearly took my head off with a *jordan mawashi geri (upper round-house* kick). It would have sent me straight to the morgue if it landed!

For his first fifty fights, Masada smashed through everyone, dropping his opponents with body rips thanks to his number one weapon, brutal round house kicks to the stomach. But his onslaught from these early fights sapped his energy and caused him a lot of damage.

By the time I fought him again later in the rounds, it was a different story. In my 100-Man Fight documentary, I showed a clip of him in those late rounds, delirious, trying to bite his

Training For The 100-Man Fight

opponent when he got close enough.

Masada was in survival mode; primal – like an animal. He couldn't even punch or kick anymore, so he would scream and let out an almighty roar (*kiai*) to keep him going and use it as a source of defense. I've never seen anything like it in my entire life, and it left an impression on me which I'll never forget.

Even The Colonel with all his years of experience training professional fighters had no idea what I would need or how I should prepare myself. And only a dozen or less people on earth knew what I would be going through on that fateful day.

Unlike a tournament where two, three, or even five of us could train together as a team and all compete, this was like a tournament just for me. And it would feel like me against the world on that day. Sure, the whole school would pull together to help out the challengers, but in this case, that challenger was just me.

Where would I even get started with my training? What book could I flip open to tell me what I needed to do? What master could I call on to instruct me as to what my daily routine should be?

None of that existed. I was going to have to make up my training as I went along - and hope it was enough. Sure, I'd have a strategy, but it had to be totally different from any preparation I'd done before – that much I knew for sure.

This time, the fight would literally go on for 3.5 hours almost straight with no breaks. I knew I had to train harder and smarter than I'd ever trained before, but was it going to be enough? Or, would I end up breaking down and going primal like Masuda or the many others who had given it a valiant effort but fallen short?

Only time would tell.

At the outset, I completely changed my mentality about training. Instead of short bursts of intense action, I actually tried to think like a marathon runner. That went contrary to everything I had been taught in karate and all my training since being a teenager. But I saw it was the real key to success.

Let's start with what's understood about the 100-man *Kumite*: it's been described as like running a marathon, but 100 competitors are running in the opposite direction, towards you. Oh, and they also happen to be punching and kicking you as hard as they can as they go past, which takes a few minutes at a time. Although it's a metaphor, that's a pretty literal physical equivalent and exactly what it feels like.

So, for 3.5 hours, I was going to be kicking and punching 100 of the best black belt competitors from all over Japan, trying not just to survive but to win each fight. At the same time, these opponents would be punching and kicking me thousands of times in return. They would be fresh, where I had to fight all of them. And the one and ONLY way I would come out victorious was if I didn't get knocked out, injured, dropped to the mat, or pass out even for an instant. If, by some incredible twist of fate, I was still standing (and still breathing) at the end, only then would I have accomplished the legendary 100-man *Kumite* and add my name to the pantheon.

So, let's get back to my preparation. Normally my training

would start about seven weeks out. But Anton and his film crew came to Thailand 16 weeks before the event to capture my preparation, a little early in my training process for my liking, coming for the month of July. Anton's crew included J.R., Ben (Hangover!), and Louis on film cameras, his brother Nick and friend Mack on sound, and Big Tommy, the professional still photographer. Looking at the big picture now, I'm actually very happy it did start that early - and with such intensity.

In that month, there were a number of people who helped me get the ball rolling. Of course, The Colonel the ever-present drill sergeant; Mohammad "Double Tap" Bahrami, my Iranian brother in arms; Nick Kara, the most skilled boxing teacher on the planet; Cris Brown, one the best Olympic wrestlers of the past 20 years and his student, Jordan; Vivien, the French ice hockey player; Mutt, the super Muay Thai boxing trainer, and of course, the entire WKO student body who I can't mention individually for fear of missing some. Mong was unfortunately not there, as he was in America for a year teaching Muay Thai. I had a great strong team behind me and I was going to need it.

My training reached a new level of intensity right from the beginning. I put high expectations upon myself, wanting to get out of my comfort zone as much as possible. I knew that during the *Kumite* I was going to be so fatigued and uncomfortable that it would take a superhuman effort to keep going, so I wanted to be prepared, mentally and physically, for that feeling. By having trained under those conditions already, I could operate on pure instinct when I faced the greatest opposition. As they say, we don't rise to the level of our expectations, but fall to the level of our training.

When Anton and his four-man crew arrived in late June, The Colonel wanted to get some good footage, so we went straight into the hardest of hard-core training. In the beginning, it was pretty similar to what I might do in the lead up to a tournament. However, the emphasis was on cardio, stamina, strength, and power to build up a solid base. We did a lot of conditioning, but not as much actual fighting in the beginning.

I started again with my Monday to Friday triple sessions, rest on Saturday, and weights on Sunday. The difference was (particularly with the cameras around) we did a lot of drills that looked spectacular but put me through a whole world of pain! Although it was so early in the training, I didn't mind because that was something required to build up the base I needed.

The mornings were as before: a mixture of slow jogs, intense hill sprints, and interval training on the bike or rowing machine. The afternoon was really where the torture began.

The Colonel came in on every one of these afternoon sessions. With our rather large support crew of WKO team members and visitors, The Colonel devised all manner of different ways to push my stamina, strength, and power. You could say that at this stage, he was trying to break me.

But I'm proud to say that even with the very extreme training and him pushing me as hard as I'd ever been pushed, he never succeeded. I withstood it all. I also ate a ton of food each day to replace all the calories I spent as best as I could. Even then, it was hard to rest properly since the build-up of lactic acid hindered me getting the best night's sleep each night.

Some of the drills that we filmed included running with 60 kilos logs, doing bunny hops up and down the dojo with the log on my shoulder. (In fact, we used this log for many different types of torturous exercises.)

But The Colonel's favorite was standing over the top of the log, bracing himself on it. Then, he would launch himself into the air and propel down with the log straight into my guts, which made my rib cage feel like it was going to explode.

The Colonel didn't hold back. But through it all, I knew this was the exact punishment my body needed. Aside from the obvious physical strength and cardio fitness, it's also vital to have strong hands and iron-like shins for full contact karate over 100 fights. These are your tools and only weapons, so if they are damaged, you won't be able to strike correctly or even defend.

So, I spent a lot of time strengthening my hands, wrists, feet, and shins. I'd kick into a solid bag filled with sand, hitting with the top of the foot and shin, numbing the nerves and calcifying the bones, turning them into weapons that would make Wolverine envious. Over and over again, for hundreds of repetitions each day, I'd strike into the log with the blade of my hand as well, trying to turn them as hard as swords. The knuckles and forearms, too, were tools that had to be sharpened for battle.

When your shins and fists are as hard as iron, it doesn't matter what you hit, you never have to pull your punches or kicks in fear of hurting yourself. You can smash through anything that's in your way, using your limbs as battering rams. I was aware that during the 100-man *Kumite*, I would not be wearing any shin guards or hand gloves – just pure bare knuckle. I'd say that *Kyokushin* fighters have the strongest bodies, without a doubt. Even a lightweight fighter can take an incredible amount of damage – or dish out punishment, like my brother, Double Tap. Therefore, I knew that over 100 fights, body conditioning and stamina would be key.

There was a hill close by my house there in Thailand that I would run twice a week, The Hill of Death, I called it. I could gauge where my stamina was with this torturous hill. It was approximately 80 meters, or 262 feet, with a steep incline to the top. When I started my training, I could do only five sprints at 100 percent. I would sprint to the top, walk back down to the bottom, then hit it again straight away, always trying to improve on my time. My goal was to be able to do 16 sprints at 100 percent, with the last sprint just as fast as the first one. As you might guess, I had a love-hate relationship with this hill, but it sure kept me honest!

I found that the rowing machine combined with heavy bag work really sharpened my cardio and made me fit, too. On the rowing machine, I'd go for one-minute intervals with 30 seconds rest in between keeping the intensity at about 70-80 percent. My goal was to get to 300 meters in one minute, rest for 30 seconds, then immediately start hitting the bag. I would do 20 sets of these, alternating between running up the hill or this rower-and-bag work on alternate days.

Nick Kara and The Colonel both pushed me hard on the pads and body shield. Nick was methodical in technique, perfecting every part of the fight game and striving only for the best. Double Tap and I would stand toe-to-toe while he just laid into me for a round at a time, either punching me in the chest and stomach or kicking me in the thighs and stomach. Really, I was trying to transform my body into a machine that could take any form of punishment, building an unbreakable shield.

A lot of people have this misconception that technique is the most important thing in a fight. But really, heart, determination, conditioning, power and stamina are all important. Of course, the best fighters in the world have amazing technique and skill, but this usually doesn't determine who is a champion. When it comes down to it, what separates the champions from the rest is their grit, their will to win, and their ability to absorb an incredible amount of pain and keep going.

Anton and the crew left at the end of July to film some interviews in Australia and get the Australian media onboard. At that stage, my training switched into a different gear. Still twelve weeks from the day of the *Kumite*, I knew I had to alter my training to concentrate more on endurance and longevity. In order to do this, I devised exercises where I would train for longer and longer periods of time, but at a lower level of intensity than that first month.

For example, I was previously doing pad work in the ring at full intensity for, say, six three-minute rounds each session. But you have to understand that the 100-man *Kumite* is a three-and-a-half-hour event without breaks, so it wasn't going to be possible to go at 100 percent intensity the whole time.

If I continued to train the same way like it was any other tournament, I wouldn't be prepared for the day of the Kumite. Instead, I wanted to replicate how the event would unfold. So, I began doing things like hitting the heavy bag at about 70 percent intensity for upwards of an hour, with say ten-second breaks every four to five minutes for a quick sip of water before going straight back into it. The punching was very basic, no combinations just straight punches into the heavy bag, *left, right, left, right,* continuously trying to keep the same tempo and power for one hour. My hands became numb from all the punching, my shoulders burned from all the lactic acid build up, and my mind would scream in pain, telling me to stop.

It was easy for my mind to wander. Instead, I had to stay focused and relaxed for a long period of time. Because it's so hot in Thailand at that time of year, the top floor gym at WKO would easily reach 40° Celsius, or 104° F. After an hour of training, there would be a pool of sweat a meter in diameter around me. I must have lost two kilos of sweat just from this one exercise.

I remember Junior (The Colonel's son) joining me in one of these drills once, and we both went at two different heavy bags for an hour. I remember looking up at him midway through and we both started laughing at how surreal this training was. God only knows what the casual gym members who were unaware of my quest were thinking.

After an hour of bag work, I would then usually follow up with another half hour in the ring just shadow boxing. This was very important to keep me focused. Then, I would get a few of the bigger guys to push back against me sumo style so I could get that feeling of having so many fighters putting pressure on me and getting used to that weight. The *Kumite* would bring a constant supply of fresh fighters, and I was the only one who was not going to be resting.

At that time in the WKO, Mong wasn't around as I mentioned. So, the only person of that standard that I needed for pure karate drills, fighting, and conditioning was my good mate Double Tap. I can't thank him enough for those months of training we did together. His contribution to my preparation cannot be overstated.

As we got closer to the event, we started doing more sparring, and just kept up with that conditioning. Anyone who is unfamiliar with this level of *Kyokushin* karate and sees these conditioning drills for the first time is pretty shocked. But every day, I would have DT literally kick and punch me literally as hard as he could while I just stood there and took it. Even though he only weighs 72 kilos, or 160 lbs., anyone who knows DT knows that he hits harder and sharper than a heavyweight. As I mentioned before, he won the heavyweight division of the All Okinawa in 2010 and was the Iranian champion.

I treated this wild period as a kind of science experiment, but I was both the scientist and the test subject. I used all my years of knowledge and experience to devise the best possible methodology to complete this ultimate challenge. People also would have been alarmed at my diet. Since I was training so many times and for so long each day, I just couldn't get enough calories. I ate double doses of porridge, morning and night, the usual Thai chicken, fish, meat, rice and vegetables, and loads of coffee, donuts and chocolate bars in between training sessions. At night once I'd finished the last session, I would go to the same restaurant and order sometimes two full meals like a huge bowl of pasta and a chicken and vegetable dish, then top it all off by eating a huge bowl of apple pie drowned in custard and ice-cream, much to the amusement of the restaurant staff, who lined up and laughed as they handed my plates down the line. By this stage it was usually about 10-11 at night, and with my stomach full and body refueled, I would go home to sleep so I could start it all again the next day.

But even after all of this, sometimes I'd eat again when I got home, just before I went to sleep. I'd force down another bowl of oatmeal with some chocolate sprinkled on it, just to carb load for the next day's training.

I remember at the time the Tour De France was on TV, and I watched a program about these cyclists who rode for six hours a day, three weeks straight. I wondered what their food intake must be like in order to do that. The TV reporter explained that they would eat up to 10,000 calories a day, so I committed myself to doing the same. I saw these elite cyclists eating massive meals in the morning and then even bigger meals in the evening, just shoveling in huge amounts of food to get through the next day. Of course, they also ate while they were cycling, but this was generally energy drinks and energy bars, chocolate bars and bananas, similar to the energy snacks I chowed in between classes.

Aside from the training and diet, part of my science experiment was how I could best recover from each day's tortuous training. For the entire four months, I had a full Thai massage for an hour to an hour and a half every day, sometimes even twice a day. This was crucial to get the lactic acid out of my body and give my muscles a better chance of relaxing and recovering. I would also go to a local Tony's Gym and jump in the ice tubs they had there as a form of cold-water recovery.

My theory has always been to train as hard as you can, go in confident that you couldn't have done any more, and then leave it all on the mat. And I have to say that in the months leading up to October 22, 2011, I'd never trained so hard in my life. If you had asked me a year earlier if it was possible to train harder than I just had for my world tournament, I probably would have said no.

But in 2011, I shattered all records. I can't think of anyone – in any sport, anywhere in the world - training harder or more intense than I did for this one event. But there's a reason martial arts people call the 100-man *Kumite,* the ultimate challenge of the spirit, and so many strong, incredibly well-trained men have failed at it. No matter the outcome, I was certainly not going to walk away with regrets that I should have trained harder.

And by mid-October 2011, I was ready.

I'd reached the peak of my life's training. I was the fittest and strongest I'd ever been, physically and mentally, before attempting the 100-man *Kumite*. I'd trained tirelessly, at unprecedented levels for months, altered my methods to scientific precision, and was 100 percent ready for the marathon of fighting that was coming. Everyone in the gym had dug deep to help me get to this point, and they would all be fighting alongside me in spirit.

Now it was time to get on the plane to Osaka, Japan, and get to work.

Just 100 fights to go.

CHAPTER 22: AFTER THE FIGHT

浪人

"Try to do exactly as you are taught without complaining or quibbling."

--Gichin Funakoshi

I successfully completed the 100-man *Kumite*. It was grueling beyond anything I'd even imagined, but all my hard training had paid off. (For a more detailed account of that 100-man fight, check out my first book, The Young Lions.)

People sometimes ask me, "How long did it take you to prepare for it?" I used to tell them "four months of intensive training," or something similar. But, looking back, it actually took me over 25 years, since that first day I walked into the Brunswick Dojo as an eager 12-year-old.

All my life I'd been preparing for the 100-man *Kumite*, whether I'd known it or not. Still to this day, it's something difficult for me to recount because when I think about it, all I remember is the pain. But, it also was a great experience that I'll never forget.

The Young Lions book tells the story of that day, and I'm thankful to be able to pick up the story from where we left off as you read this.

The day after I completed the 100-man fight, I was invited to be the guest of honor and sit alongside Kancho Sugihara at a huge kid's tournament held in the main stadium. In Japan, karate is like football in the West and millions practice the form. The Byakuren kids tournaments are well attended and incredibly well run, and this one was no exception.

I went up to my hotel room around about 11 p.m. the night before. By then, the adrenaline was fading, replaced by agonizing pain throughout my body. My legs, arms, torso - and anywhere that was a target for the thousands of blows I took from my opponents that day - was in screaming pain.

I didn't sleep at all that night. Instead, I spent half the night vomiting, urinating and defecating an endless stream of unrecognizable black liquid. There was no doctor present, so I can't give you a scientific explanation - but let's just say it wasn't pleasant.

World Champion Kenji Yamaki, in an interview about his 100-man *Kumite* in 1995, said "I felt like I would die. My whole body was affected. I was taken to the emergency room at the hospital and the doctor said I looked like I'd been in a car accident — like I'd been hit by a truck. My kidneys were damaged. I lost

After The Fight

consciousness and almost died."

At about 10 a.m., however, I put on my nice blue suit, put on my best poker face, and walked down to the stadium. Approximately 500 kids were fighting that day, and there must have been 5,000 relatives and spectators in attendance.

Sugihara was very kind to place me at the head of the official's table beside him. As the tournament commenced, he announced my achievement the day before to the entire crowd. Anton tells me that the whole stadium erupted in applause, but I must have been a bit groggy and out of sorts because my memory of that is patchy.

Sugihara also assigned me the honor of bestowing the winning trophies to the kids, and he also announced that they could have their karate *dogis* signed by me if they wished. I must have signed all 500 *dogis* by the end of the day. It's not customary, so I felt honored to do this and see the smiles on the kids' faces. I'd actually never seen someone sign a karate *dogi* before, so I guess it was a symbol of how proud Sugihara was of my achievement.

Since I was invited to sit at the head table alongside Sugihara, I made sure to hide my pain behind a smile, managing to hold it for the entire day. Two of my students were competing, so I spent some of the time coaching them when their fights came up. I was awed by the whole day's events and managed to block out the pain for most of the time. To top it off, my student, Minto, won the female 15-year-old division and I couldn't have been prouder of her.

As the kids tournament progressed, the pain grew worse by the minute. My poker face must have been pretty good because the guys remarked as to how normal I was looking - and how surprised they were at my recovery. I can only think it was adrenaline that was still keeping me going.

Anton and the crew were still filming scenes for the documentary and there was work to be done. They wanted to return to Tokyo and the old *Kyokushin Honbu*. That was fine with me since I had a couple of days off, and my mum and friends went via Kyoto while Mo and I took the direct route to Tokyo.

Hour by hour, however, I was getting progressively worse. By Monday, the pain in my legs, hands and forearms was particularly excruciating, right when I had to catch the bullet train to Tokyo. It was so agonizing that for the first two days in Tokyo, I barely got out of bed. I was definitely a different person than at the Sunday kids tournament, where it seemed that I would walk away with little or no after-effects. Reality had set in, like I had a delayed reaction to the trauma I experienced on Saturday.

My legs were black and swollen all over. I had massive amounts of fluid retention. My forearms and hands were smashed and totally bruised and bloodied. And I was still pissing and crapping that same mysterious black liquid. We even took photos of my blackened legs a couple of days later for the scrap book.

I really should have been in a hospital and on strong pain killers, but this being Japan and such a rare event, it was just an oversight that a doctor wasn't present. It had been about five

After The Fight

years since the last 100-man *Kumite*, and probably would be another five until the next.

It was no-one's fault, really, but it sure didn't help me that day! So, in the spirit of *Kyokushin*, I just dealt with the pain and kept going without complaint. *Osu!*

CHAPTER 23: REFLECTIONS

浪人

"Karate is the most Zen-like of all the martial arts. It has abandoned the sword. This means that it transcends the idea of winning and losing to become a way of thinking and living for the sake of other people in accordance with the way of Heaven. Its meaning, therefore, reach the profoundest levels of human thought."

--Mas Oyama

By Wednesday, my third day in Tokyo, Anton, my family, and a few friends had arrived. I was starting to feel good again after two days mostly in bed. Being back in my old stomping ground from my *uchi deshi* days, I felt drawn to the *Honbu* in Ikebukuro. So, Anton, the film crew, and I made our way there via Tokyo's subway system. It was surreal after being away for so long. Just traveling through Tokyo brought back so many memories.

The old *Honbu* is not used much anymore but is still sort of a shrine to Sosai and his achievements. His daughter, Kuristina, kept the dojo in exactly the same condition as it was when I left 20 years earlier. Of course, we called ahead to let her know we were coming.

Kuristina was there when we arrived and knew I had completed the 100-man *Kumite* a few days earlier. She was quite emotional that one of her father's last students had completed his ultimate challenge, particularly at the age of 40. We talked for a few minutes in the foyer about the old days. She was often present with her father at the *Honbu* and occasionally for a meal at the dormitory, so she knew all of the *uchi deshi* from the last few years very well.

Kuristina told me that she and her husband now held only kids classes a couple of times a week. She shared with me that she still hoped *Kyokushin* might one day be unified again. Her father was such a powerful personality and his passing seemed to have been a pivotal moment in all of our lives. That was equally true for his daughter, Kuristina, and his surrogate sons, the Young Lions. Kuristina was as overwhelmed by the situation as I was, so I took the opportunity to ask permission to enter the old dojo for a look around. She said, "*Dozo, onegaishimau* - Please go ahead," so we took our shoes off and went inside.

I remember climbing the old, tiled stairs of the *Honbu*, stepping onto the wooden floor of the dojo on the 2nd floor, and thinking how nothing had changed. Certainly nothing had changed about the whole outside facade of the building. In fact, the whole neighborhood seemed somehow frozen in time. The inside, too, was like a museum. All the old pictures on the walls, Sosai's awards and accolades, the old Shinto shrine, the training hall itself, even the tennis balls hanging from the ceiling by strings were exactly as I remembered. But, like *Kyokushin* around the world, outside of general appearances, perhaps everything had changed.

What was most obvious was the lack of any activity or noise. I remember when I was last there, hundreds of bodies were coming and going - students training, *kiai*-ing, *osu*-ing, bowing, and preparing for all manner of camps, events, and tournaments. It seemed that when Sosai died, he took the soul of the *Honbu* with him. His spirit and teachings live on, of course. *Kyokushin* in its many forms is still a very strong fighting art, just in a different way from when Sosai was our one great leader.

I walked through the familiar rooms, trying to make sense of what I had done, while the crew filmed some for the documentary. I found myself emotional from the gravity of the experience. Nothing could prepare me for the sense of familiarity; the sights and smells and feel of this beautiful old building; all of the great memories that had led me to that very moment.

But I also didn't expect it to be so quiet. I used to chuckle to myself when taking classes, thinking about what the neighbors thought of all the noise that emanated from the building, all day, every day. I'd never imagined coming back to see it so silent and empty.

Inside the dojo, there are many pictures of Sosai and his

achievements. It was quite a humbling experience to return to the place where I'd learned everything about karate – and life – from my one true master. It had been almost fifteen years since I had last been there, but it may as well have been 150 years. The *Honbu* was like a time capsule. Absolutely everything was exactly in the same place as it was before, but what was missing were the people, the heart and soul of *Kyokushin* karate.

I still felt Sosai's presence, but it felt somewhat hollow and empty without him there anymore. I reminisced about being there with Nick, Yamagake, Kuruda, Komukai and all the other *uchi deshi* and outside students. But that may as well have been 1,000 years ago. People had moved on and had families and careers. Most stuck with their karate, or used it to progress forward in life, and many were now high-ranking branch chiefs. But that golden era had come to a close.

Looking around the *Honbu* at all the pictures of Sosai, I was quite emotional, and I was taken aback by the enormity of the moment. I must admit that I didn't give the film crew the greatest of interviews, as I was somewhat at a loss for words. But I was very happy to be standing there as one of Sosai's last Young Lions, and one of the few who had conquered the two achievements he always told us to strive for.

I'd reached both the pinnacle of fighting *and* completed the 100-man *Kumite*. I'm sure Sosai imagined I might achieve that in a unified world of *Kyokushin* karate. But, then again, as *Kyokushin* broke apart after his death and then splintered and evolved, so had I.

Reflections

In the 20 years since I'd left this building, I'd trained and fought under many full-contact styles and had consistently fought the best fighters, always coming close to winning each championship I entered. I got so much from my time with Sosai – many life lessons that can never be taken away. But one of the most impactful was the will and determination he taught me, to fight against all odds and never give up in the face of adversity until I had achieved my ultimate goal. Coming back to the place where I learnt the true meaning of the spirit of *Osu*, I had done just that.

As I walked through the dojo that day, I hoped Sosai was looking down, proud of me. I stood in the shrine, taking a quiet moment in front of the large bronze picture of Sosai. If I listened hard enough, I could almost hear him speaking to me once again in his typical booming Sosai voice, "Mmmmm, subarashii yo, sugoi yo Juddo - Mmmmm, well done Judd, good job."

CHAPTER 24:
THE BROTHERS REUNITE

浪人

I'm not in this world to live up to your expectations and you're not in this world to live up to mine.

--Bruce Lee

The next day was our last full day in Tokyo. Anton arranged through Nick Pettis for us to visit the offices of my third brother in arms, The Pink Panther, Yamakage San. At this stage, Nick was working for him in some capacity, so he arranged for the three of us to get together in the afternoon. I'd heard that Yamakage had become a very successful businessman and the owner of a number of companies, with his head office in a modern skyscraper in Roppongi in the center of Tokyo.

We met at a quiet restaurant near his office; Nick, me, and the Pink Panther back together again. I was still exhausted from the *100-Man Fight* but eager to reunite with my long-lost third brother in arms. It had been 18 years and since I had last seen him.

I remember standing there waiting and feeling so excited when I saw him arrive with Nick. Straight away I went up to the Pink Panther and hugged him saying, "Long time no see, Yamakage San!!" I gave Nick a hug as well. I was just so happy for the three of us to be together again after all the years.

Yamakage took charge and said, let's go inside and eat. We sat down and I think for the first five minutes we all had big grins on our faces, making small talk and just enjoying each other's presence.

The Pink Panther looked as smooth as ever. He hadn't aged at all, with the same wry smile on his face I always remembered. He wasn't as muscular as he once was, but was dressed to the nines, looking very sharp. Cooler than cool, in fact.

He asked me how I had been all these years and I told him that I'd been training and teaching the whole time, and just completed the 100-man *Kumite*. Of course, he knew that, and he asked how I felt, if I was injured and all okay?

I was actually in severe pain, but I was over the moon to be with my brothers, so I said, "All is good Yamakage San." He was happy to see me and the three of us sat there eating, talking, and joking around just like the old days.

When we finished our lunch, the Pink Panther took us to his office. His staff met us at the entrance to the building, fussing over us and bowing before taking us up the elevator to his offices. The Pink Panther hadn't changed his style one bit. But now he was the boss, so he had people running around after him like

The Brothers Reunite

they were his *kohais*, or juniors, in karate. By the look of things, he had become a powerful man – a force to be reckoned with.

So, here was the Pink Panther running a huge business on an entire floor of one of the most expensive real estate blocks in the world. His office was miraculous. There were marbled floors, a huge entrance decked out with the names of all of his companies, and people running everywhere. From what I could see, he must have had 100 staff working for him at that location alone.

The Pink Panther had become what he wanted to be and climbed to the top in his chosen way of life. It was always going to turn out that way for the Pink Panther.

When Anton and the film crew arrived, the Pink Panther was kind enough to let us use one of his offices to film some interviews. Nick, the Pink Panther, and I sat down and talked about old times and our days as *uchi deshi*. Part of it was recorded for the documentary, but we left the camera off for much of the conversation.

Not everything was for the public, as we harkened back to being those three fresh-faced kids who'd beaten the odds and survived the toughest fighting school for *karateka* in the world. And now, here we were: Nick the K1 champion and host of one of the most popular TV shows on NHK Japan, the Pink Panther, the millionaire businessman, and me, the lifetime *karateka*.

We talked a lot about Sosai and the old days. The Pink Panther joked about a time I got him in trouble somehow and he had to do jumping squats under orders from Yui, the Ranger, for an entire night. Nick talked about his recent TV series on martial arts called "Samurai Spirit" and his life in Japan as the Blue-Eyed Samurai. We all really enjoyed the moment.

Kyokushin karate, and our time as Young Lions, had shaped us into the people we were that day, and only we knew just how strong an influence Sosai had on our lives.

Later on, for our last night in Tokyo, Anton organized a dinner at Gonpachi, a well-known, traditional Japanese restaurant in the middle of the city. It was often referred to as the "Kill Bill restaurant," since movie producer Quentin Tarantino modeled the restaurant in his movie of the same title. Since the restaurant's owner had refused his request to close to the public so they could film there, Tarantino instead constructed a detailed replica for his final fight scene.

A large group of family and old friends were out that night - perhaps 20 in total - and we all enjoyed that one final golden moment before returning to the real world. It was a great night, one that none of us will ever forget. It was our one last chance for the brothers of *Kyokushin* to reunite, but I hope there's another opportunity for us all to meet up again soon.

CHAPTER 25: RETURN TO AUSTRALIA AND THE DOCUMENTARY RELEASE

浪人

"A human life gains luster and strength only when it is polished and tempered."

--Mas Oyama

At the end of 2012, for the first time in many years, I felt the pull to return to Australia. I had been dating my serious girlfriend, Mothana, for four years at that time. We visited Australia for a holiday in the middle of the year, and I got the chance to introduce "Mo" too all my family and friends. Mo and I were considering the idea of having children of our own, the documentary was building up hype for a 2013 release, and it seemed the logical next step to return to Australia and start my own dojo. All my life I'd worked for different teachers and gym owners, but now I felt strongly that it was time to do my own thing. It didn't hurt that

Australia was the strongest it had been economically in a long while, so I thought, let's go back and give it a shot.

We arrived a week before Christmas (summer in Australia), and summer is always a great time there. My good mate, Russ, organized an apartment for me in my old stomping grounds of inner-city Footscray. Within weeks I was able to open up a small gym nearby. Without any advertising at all we quickly picked up a stack of kids and a fair number of adults, and I tried to settle back into Australian life as best I could. But, after spending more than half my adult life living in Asia, that wasn't as easy as I'd anticipated.

Anton's documentary was really gaining momentum at this point and I was fielding hundreds of calls and emails asking when it was coming out. Anyone who's ever made a film understands how long the editing process takes, so in the meantime, Anton started a Facebook page and website to keep people informed.

The film's release was picked up by both the Australian and overseas press. As the release date drew closer, we had TV, radio, and Internet media all over the film. The Australian press loved the story of a local boy doing good, and we were picked up by *The Huffington Post*, *Cracked*, and some huge UFC blogs and online publications in the United States. They even likened my 100-man *Kumite* to the Frank Dux story about a mythical *Kumite* staged in Hong Kong that was a knock-out tournament between various martial artists. The story was eventually made into the 1988 film *Bloodsport* starring Jean Claude Van Damme. Of course, my *Kumite* was completely different from this Hollywood fictionalized version, but it sure didn't hurt with publicity. By the time of our documentary's release, interest from the public was at fever pitch.

Journey to the 100-Man Fight premiered at Melbourne's grand old Astor Theatre in August 2013 to a sell-out crowd. I was thrilled that Anton's film, and the spectacle of what I'd done, really blew the public away. People queued up for two hours ,100 meters down the street on either side of the cinema, just to get good seats before the doors opened. We had a number of sponsors come onboard who offered ticket holders free food and drinks. We also printed hundreds of posters and promotional tee-shirts and everything sold out quickly.

The reaction to the film was more than I ever expected – it really surprised me. So many people were inspired and amazed at what I had done. For the first time in my life, the general public outside of the karate world was able to see inside my world and what I'd achieved.

I was featured on three different TV programs in the lead-up, and Mark "Hammer" Catstagnini, a famous commentator and kickboxing show host from Fox Sports, was kind enough to agree to emcee the whole event. Mark used to train karate with me at the St. Kilda Dojo, so he had a personal insight into my history and fighting career.

We had a Q&A after the film, with most of the people who appeared in the film on stage fielding questions and Hammer moderating. Sitting up on the grand stage were my mum, Shihan Eddie, Anton, Cris Brown, Dr. Peter Lewis and, of course, me.

My old teacher, Shihan Eddie, who is now in his late 80s, can tell quite a story and had the crowd in stitches. The Q&A went for about an hour and a half, but still, nobody wanted to leave. They all just wanted to hear about what I had done and what it was like for me. I am not an accomplished public speaker by any measure, and as a *karateka* we are taught to be humble and unassuming, so I was surprised to feel very comfortable talking about my life. That was just the first of many screenings and Q&As to come that year.

It was an incredible afternoon and evening, and after the Q&A finished, people stayed around for a drink and something to eat as I signed posters and tee-shirts until the end. There was this amazing buzz and I didn't want it to go away. The management at the Astor said they hadn't hosted an event like that in over 20 years with such an electric atmosphere, so I guess Anton didn't do such a bad job with the film!

We had about ten screenings in Australia and were invited to another ten film festivals overseas, winning some awards in the USA and headlining the TILT film festival, Australia's largest independent national film festival. I have to say that it was a lot of fun, and we were asked to go to schools and business functions for even more screenings. I was fielding numerous offers for public speaking engagements and was planning on holding seminars around the world.

There was only one problem with all of this – and it really

came out of left field. During my career, I had a lot of luck avoiding serious injuries, unlike your average fighter. Perhaps the most troubling injuries I can remember were breaking bones in my hand and fracturing my ribs a few times, but nothing really debilitating. And it never took more than a few months to fully recover.

But not long after arriving in Australia, I began to notice a nagging pain in my left hip, like when you injure your groin and it takes forever to heal and never goes away. I did have one major injury from the 100-man *Kumite*, a quadricep muscle that literally tore off my knee and retracted into my leg. I had seen Dr. Peter Lewis, a renowned sports physician I'd known for many years, about this. He told me that this was one of four quadricep muscles and although I may never have 100% strength in that leg again, having three other perfectly fine muscles, it would never really hinder me to any great extent.

At the time, I thought this hip pain may have been connected to that injury. However, my hip didn't improve over the coming months. I found that in my new role as teacher at my own school, I was limited in my movement, which hindered me from doing my job. So, I went back to Dr. Lewis and had some X-rays and an MRI done. They showed that the left hip joint had basically worn out from years and years of kicking. The cartilage was almost completely gone, and the joint was rubbing almost bone on bone. The only solution was a full hip replacement. At only 41 years old and with a long recovery time, I was devastated by this prognosis at first.

In retrospect, this is not an uncommon injury for karate practitioners. Nick Pettas already had both hips replaced and he wasn't even 40.

With Australia being as expensive as it is (and me having no health insurance), I decided to wait it out and see if alternative therapies would have some effect. Even the doctors suggested this option since the operation was going to cost in the vicinity of $40,000. I was more than happy to try a cheaper option first!

But over the course of the 18 months I was in Australia, the injury didn't get any better. If anything, it got worse and really impacted my job as a karate teacher. I enjoyed running my own school, but my style has always been to lead by example. But now, I couldn't do this, and I have to admit that it stole some of my joy. For example, if students were going to do 50 push-ups, I would always do 60. If they were going to do 100 sit ups, I would do 120. That's just my style and the way I'll always be. I guess I picked that up from Sosai, who was teaching classes until the very end. I'm not the sort of person to delegate to a second, and I hope to be physically fit into my 80s or longer, still training students this way. But for the first time in my life, I couldn't do that.

Despite my injury, it wasn't all bad in Australia. Through my old mate, Michael Dugina, I was offered a job as a fitness coach at the Essendon Football Club. For anyone who lives outside of Australia, the Australian Football League, or AFL, is by far the most watched professional sports organization in Australia. The AFL generates billions of dollars in revenue each year and

Return To Australia And The Documentary Release

is watched by nearly everyone - you could call it the NFL of Australia.

My role at the football club was as their Boxing and Conditioning Trainer, working primarily with the younger players. Although they were pro athletes, they looked more like baby-faced kids to me, since I was 40 and they were all in their early 20s. So, it was a great experience, and really opened my eyes to see what the inside of a professional sports club looks like, as the facilities and coaching at that level are world class.

Training for professional footballers is really like science these days. They have coaches for just about everything including psychologists, sports movement scientists, dietitians, doctors... and this is where I came in. I was there to give them an alternative type of fitness, getting the players out of their comfort zone and bringing them back to reality. The coach, Mark Thompson, told me directly, "Don't go easy on the boys, push them and make them work hard." I certainly did that.

We did a lot of drills that I used to do in karate like lining them up to punch each other bare knuckles to the body, pushing them hard on the pads, and wrestling, throwing them around. They certainly weren't used to it, but they really enjoyed the training and got a lot out of it. I hoped that it helped give them that 1 or 2 percent edge that can be the difference between winning and losing in football. I really enjoyed working there.

On July 10th, 2014, the biggest event in my life occurred. Mo and my dream came true when she gave birth to our baby son,

Max Milin Reid. I was present at Max's birth and it was a powerful experience. He came out a big, healthy baby boy with a big ET-like head but covered in blood, mucus and membrane, looking like an alien from some outer world. I was happier than I've ever been, and so was Mo.

We'd been trying to have a baby for a couple of years at that point, so Max was a huge blessing, our own son, part of the two of us. Now we were truly a family. It hit me like a ton of bricks that my life was never going to be the same again, but in a great way. Max's birth was the happiest day of my life and was to be yet another turning point in the direction we would take. Things happen for a reason, and Max's arrival was going to show me the way to true peace and fulfillment.

CHAPTER 26: FAMILY AND BACK WHERE I BELONG

浪人

"Until the day I die, I never want to be separated from my dogi. I never want to cease my training efforts in the dojo."

--Mas Oyama

About the time Max was born, my hip injury was at its worst. It had degenerated to the point that I could barely walk, let alone train karate. Although I was feeling elated about Max, I was very down about my inability to teach and do what I love. Even working with the football club was becoming more difficult. They knew about my injury and even paid for a specialist to give me the best treatment possible, but it wasn't having any effect.

Living in Thailand for six years, I had often seen advertising for medical procedures done at the local Thai hospitals. Unbeknownst to most outsiders, the medical care in Thailand is world class. Countless foreigners fly in just for medical treatment, which is referred to as medical tourism. Procedures are often less than half the price of what they cost in many western countries and from my experience living there, the doctors are first rate. Not to mention, the waiting lists to have surgeries are usually just weeks instead of the two or three years like with the public health system in Australia. After a little research, I found out one of the main procedures most commonly done are joint replacements - hips and knees, as well as dental work and cosmetic surgery.

By September, I was hesitant to even hold Max and walk with him for fear that my hip would fail and I'd drop him. This really lit a fire under me, and I resolved to fix the injury that was dragging me down – physically as well as mentally - as soon as possible.

Once I made that decision, it all happened quickly. Mo and I canceled the lease on our apartment, put our belongings in storage, and headed straight back to Thailand. Thankfully, we'd held onto our house over there in a nice part of Chon Buri nearby Jomtien Beach, about two hours from Bangkok. The house is a large place with four bedrooms and a swimming pool, much more spacious than the apartment we were living in Melbourne. Returning to Thailand with its warm weather, easy going people, and festival-like atmosphere on the streets felt like we were returning to paradise.

Within two weeks, I was booked into Paria Thai #3 Hospital in Bangkok. After just a few hours of surgery, I had had my old, worn-out hip replaced with a brand-new titanium, metal, and ceramic hip. To my utter amazement, I was walking on it the next day.

But after the operation, I wasn›t 100 percent sure that I›d be able to train karate again.

When I asked a few people who'd had their hips replaced before, I got some bad feedback, as most of them said I'd never be able to kick again. My hopes for a full recovery waned.

That hit me hard. After all, I had no income, no job on the horizon, and all I'd done my whole life was train and teach karate. Our funds were starting to dry up and I had a family now.

All of this played heavily on my mind during my stay at the hospital in Bangkok, but I was determined to prove them wrong and get my life back.

Anton sent Hangover Ben over to Thailand to film the pre-op and post-op, documenting the whole process. Always the one with exceptional foresight, Anton wanted to make the best of the situation by filming it and then trying to tap into the medical tourism market in Thailand.

Since Ben helped with filming *Journey to the 100-Man Fight*, we thought he could piece together some good footage of me at the hospital, talking about how great Thailand's hospitals are. We didn't know how all this was going to turn out, but we thought what the hell – let's give it a try.

Thankfully, the operation went smoothly. From start to finish, I had a pleasant experience with Thailand's medical system and only have good things say (and no, I'm not in medical tourism!).

After the operation, I literally had to teach myself how to walk again. I've never been so happy to walk normally, without that agonizing pain. The physiotherapist gave me simple instructions on how to rebuild the muscles in my hip, but I wasn't satisfied with just being able to walk. I wanted to be healthy, strong, and limber enough to train to my full potential, the same as I did before.

The recovery was a long road and really taught me patience. For five solid months, I rehabbed and trained in my backyard. Literally one step at a time, from walking again within weeks, to riding a bike, slow jogs, then squatting, and finally, back at the gym.

The whole time I trained in my backyard, I listened to the soundtrack of the Quintin Tarantino movie, *Django Unchained*. I'm never one to listen to music while training or even in the gym. But at this time in my life, the song *Freedom* drove me to work harder, building my resolve to be strong again so I could kick, teach karate, and provide for Mo and Max. No matter how ridiculous I felt relearning to walk like a toddler, I was determined to get past this.

Soon, I was doing hundreds of push-ups, sit-ups and squats just as a warm-up. I started everything from the beginning, rebuilding the foundation of my life, my health, and my karate. My training was all basics, just like my early *uchi deshi* days in Japan. Shortly after, I was doing simple punch combos, and around the third month, I could slowly introduce kicking. I can't express how good it felt to be able to kick again! I was now sure that I'd be able to teach and continue my life in karate. We didn't have a cent to our names, but I was feeling super positive, free from my health concerns, and ready to take on the world once again.

Initially, we'd planned to stay only a few months, just long enough to get through the rehabilitation until we returned to Australia. But from the day I arrived back, I realized that Thailand was where I belonged at that time. Mo is Thai and so my son is half-Thai. And after all my years living there, I have to say I have become accustomed to the laid-back lifestyle. So, we decided to stay.

I didn't want to disappoint my family and students in Australia, but I truly felt that Thailand was where I belonged at the time. In that tropical Southeast Asian nation, life was a lot more relaxed than in modern Australia, as I was happiest just heading down to the beach with Max and Mo each afternoon, watching the waves lapping against the shore as the sun set.

Within six months of the hip replacement, I was almost able to train like I did before. By mid-2015, Shihan Robert Wiklund and Marcelo Hidalogo invited me to teach karate at a summer camp, so I was off to Sweden. I was still in the early days of recovery really, but I had to get on with my life and support my family. Talk about trial by fire – my new hip had no choice but to work. I had such a wonderful experience at this camp meeting new people, and I realized how much karate meant to me. I can't thank Robert Wiklund enough for organizing this and also organizing a lunch with my good old friend Goran Molin from Stockholm. This camp really got me back on track and reunited me with the fire inside once again.

Back in Thailand and feeling positive about the future, my good old mate Dean Booth came to visit me. On one particular day, we were kicking back in the pool chatting away and Dean had said why don't you run camps here in Thailand.

You could market it as Judd Reid's *uchi deshi* camps in Thailand, Dean said, giving them that *uchi deshi* experience you had in Japan. I was a little unsure at the start, but the more Dean and I talked about it, the more it sounded possible. Dean is a great friend and always super positive. I rang Anton and told him about the camp idea. He said it sounded great. He also said let's write a book about your time in Japan, letting the world know about your incredible experience as an *uchi deshi*. A book! This all sounded new and exciting to me.

As both Dean and Anton planted the seed in my head about the camp and the book, I realized that it was another way I could give back to Kyokushin. So, I started advertising what I called the Judd Reid *uchi deshi* camps for full-contact fighters. They were open to fighters and martial artists from any style. I was non-political; everyone was welcome as long as you came with fire in your belly and you were willing to give it your best – that's all that mattered.

Family And Back Where I Belong

Once I announced my camp, the response was overwhelming. Within a short time, I pretty much filled both scheduled camps, and planned on holding them annually. The duty of a karate fighter with experience such as mine is to continue to teach. All I wanted to do was pass on the knowledge I'd learned from Sosai and 20 years of tournament fighting, continuing to do what I love.

Anton and I were planning on meeting up soon to work on the first book. Life was great and looking very promising.

CHAPTER 27: THE MEKONG RIVER

浪
人

Three months later, it was my second trip to Cambodia with Anton to work on our new book, *The Young Lions*. I needed to do a visa run to extend my stay in Thailand, so skipping next door to Cambodia made perfect sense. And we both needed a place to concentrate purely on the book with no distractions from the outside world, no family, friends, or work.

My first "book trip" to Cambodia with Anton had gone magnificently. We worked twelve hours a day on the book for two weeks straight. We would wake up about 6 a.m. and hit the gym for a quick workout. Anton and I went pretty hard, super-setting bench presses and chin ups, then finished it off with bike sprints. Even at 6 a.m., it was damn hot and humid in the midst of Phnom Penh. So, after that we'd relax in the rooftop pool for about 30 minutes, overlooking the Mekong river and beautiful Buddhist temples in the city below. Sitting in that pool with Anton afterwards, we'd just chat about life, the view of the vast river both magical and peaceful. Cambodia was such a different world compared to Thailand, let alone Australia.

Far off, across the river below was an old rundown house right on the riverbank. It was a single-story house made from simple bricks and wooden boards. It had an outdoor shower that was really just a simple spigot with a huge bucket that could be used to bathe, and a small kitchen on the side of the wall.

At the same time we were relaxing in the pool every morning, a woman would come outside and wash herself. She was wrapped in an apron and would mostly wash her face and feet, it seemed. Anton and I didn't want to seem like we were intruding on her privacy, but we couldn't help noticing her since we were on the same schedule. But, being twelve levels up and a fair distance away, I think it really didn't make a difference.

I remember seeing her each morning on the first trip, and Anton and I would comment about what a simple and peaceful life she lives. We pondered if it would be better to live in a "modern" city but working twelve hours a day, bills up to your eyeballs, and trying to keep up with the Jones' next door, or to live a simple life like this woman. I would have to say at that moment, we both chose her life.

Cambodia was indeed a very special place, a spiritual place, and this is what we needed to stir up my creativity and gain the perspective to tell my story. After this awesome start to the day, we'd hit breakfast for an all-you-can-eat western-style buffet, and then begin our work on the book.

The Mekong River

We wrote solidly for hours, bouncing back and forth with conversations, stories, and anecdotes, Anton typing away a thousand miles per hour while I spoke. If we got tired, we cranked up our energy with strong coffee and marched on. Soon, the shadows grew long on the riverside quay, and we'd crack open a few beers to break up the monotony. The story would flow even better then.

Our system worked perfectly. The staff at the restaurant were super cool and didn't mind that we spent the whole day there as long as we kept buying coffee or beers. By about 8 p.m., we were done and dusted, so we'd have a quick feed before hitting the sack and starting the whole thing again early in the morning. We were on a mission to complete the book.

One evening, I was watching cable TV in my hotel room and just about to fall asleep when Anton rang me. When I answered the phone, Anton said to turn to the movie channel – the movie Rocky was playing. Fired up, Anton said, "This is gonna be your book, mate!"

It was pretty cool to see Rocky playing, the patron saint of fighter comeback movies. Anton and I talked about that movie before coming to Cambodia, as he wanted our book to have a storyline that rivaled *Rocky*. "It's gonna be the new Rocky series!" Anton said.

He is awesome, so pumped and enthusiastic for life, I thought that night. *With him by my side, we can do anything.* The rest of the first Cambodian trip went great and we got a ton of work done.

Months later, knowing that we'd done a magnificent job our first time around, Anton and I were rapt to get back to Cambodia. With our daily system of workout-pool-writing all day-coffee (and a few beers), we were ready to finish the second draft of the book.

Returning to Cambodia in November of 2015, Anton and I jumped right into our system for a week, hitting the gym, the pool, and visiting the same restaurants. Of course, the workers and owners remembered us, and welcomed us back with warm hospitality. But we had a third member of our writing team this time – Norm Schriever, who just flew into Phnom Penh from New York and was ready to help us out with the book. Dazed by the time change and a 28-hour travel day, Norm checked into the same hotel as us and hit the rooftop gym and pool for our afternoon session.

Norm lives an incredible and interesting life. Originally from the USA, he got tired of the nine-to-five grind years ago, so he hit the road, traveling and living all over the world while he worked as a writer. He's spent years in Costa Rica, Nicaragua, Thailand, and the Philippines, and was moving full-time to Cambodia when he came to meet us and work on the book. Anton had met Norm a year earlier, coincidentally right there in Phnom Penh. A mutual Melbourne mate, Clint, knew Anton was working on the documentary and that Norm was a writer. Clint messaged them both that they should meet up while in Cambodia, and crazy enough, they happened to be staying in the same hotel that day – the Pickled Parrot.

The Mekong River

Anton was headed out that morning, so they met up around 7 a.m. for breakfast. Two of the friendliest people on the planet who would both start a conversation with anyone, they were bound to get along famously and become mates. When Anton told Norm all about the *100-Man Fight* movie and plans to turn it into a book, Norm agreed to help out any way he could, including writing up a few articles for the Huffington Post. A few months after that, I met Norm in Thailand when he came through with Clint G, and we all got along great.

Fast forward a year and Anton, Norm, and I were reunited in Cambodia, ready to get to work on something pretty extraordinary. But with almost two days of traveling without proper sleep, there wasn't going to be much work done that first night. So, we decided to head out to dinner at a local restaurant to catch up. It was nice to kick back over a good feed and then a couple of beers. I remember taking it all in, living an adventure in a wild, exotic place with my best old mate and a great new friend, thinking about how lucky I was to have them on my side and supporting me.

After a few more beers at a local watering hole, one-by-one, we went back to the hotel to call it a night. We decided to skip the morning's weight training session and meet for breakfast instead, to coffee-up and start writing.

The following morning, I woke up and made my way down for breakfast. Norm was sitting there by himself and welcomed me with a "Good morning, mate," chuckling because he was working on his Aussie slang.

"Good morning, my man," I replied back.

I joined my new friend and then helped myself to the buffet.

"Have you seen Anton yet?" I asked.

CHAPTER 28: ANTON

浪人

Norm and I waited in the restaurant, watching the door for Anton to show up at any minute. But soon, we couldn't fill up our plates anymore or keep chatting away about the book, pretending we weren't growing curious, if not yet concerned. Anton must be sleeping in, or maybe he was hungover, we guessed. Norm and I talked more until the hotel's staff started cleaning off tables and emptying out the buffet.

"Anton must be tired," I said. "I'll go and call his room."

I went down to the reception desk and called his room but there was no answer. I told Norm, and we guessed that maybe he had been up early and maybe was out taking a walk or shopping. So, we decided to do some boxing on the top floor to wait it out until Anton got back. We grabbed our focus mitts and gloves and did a quick session.

"I'll go and give Anton another call," I said to Norm afterwards.

We went back down to the reception area and tried calling his room again, but once again there was no answer.

I asked the hotel's front desk girl if they'd seen Anton that morning, but they answered no.

I was beginning to get a bit worried. Scenarios and possibilities pushed their way up into my consciousness, but I shoved them down and remained calm. Maybe he had an accident outside the night before and was hit by a car or something.

Norm and I sat in the big, comfortable chairs in the lobby for an hour or so, scanning the front door of the hotel and the elevator, waiting for Anton to turn up.

Around 1 pm, our sense of urgency dialed way up, and we couldn't pretend everything was ok anymore. I asked the front desk workers if they could open Anton's room. I thought that if his laptop was there, I knew he must be somewhere outside.

The receptionist asked us to wait a minute and we sat back down in the lobby.

After about 45 minutes the receptionist said, "You can go with the security guard, he will open the door for you. " Two other staff members joined us as we took the elevator up to Anton's floor, which I thought was strange. It was an excruciatingly silent ride to the 4th floor.

When the doors opened, Norm and I followed the hotel entourage to Anton's door. The security guy knocked several times and then unlocked and opened the door.

The lights were out but straight away I could feel the cool breeze from the air-conditioning, which was still running. I entered the room and switched on the light.

Anton was laying on the bed on his stomach, wearing his underwear and a t-shirt, his laptop computer open in front of him.

"Anton, Anton!" I called out. He didn't respond. Anton was in a sleeping position on his stomach, his arm cushioned under a pillow. I shook his leg to wake him up.

His leg was cold, which is something I've never felt on a human body before. His body was motionless as I shook his leg again. I bent down close to his face and yelled out "Anton, wake up mate!" I touched his face, and that's when my heart dropped. His eyes were half-closed, but there was no movement or breathing.

"Anton!" I screamed out loud.

But he was dead.

I quickly ran to the door and yelled, "He's dead!" Norm's face dropped with disbelief and horror.

I ran back inside the room and shook my friend, not believing this was happening.

What was going on? This can't be! Anton!

The security guy and staff asked us to leave the room. The pain and horror come down crashing on me. Norm and I were both crying in the hallway, in utter shock. My best friend Anton was gone.

I don't really remember all of what happened next, as we were in a daze. I don't remember going downstairs, but somehow found myself in the hotel's conference room, sitting at the table with Norm next to me, his head in his hands. A steady stream of police, news reporters, and other officials kept arriving into the conference room. One of the police officers, who seemed sympathetic and treated us with compassion, introduced himself and asked us some questions. He asked where we were from, what we were doing the night before, when was the last time we saw Anton or talked to him, and more.

My brain was numb. It was my worst nightmare. I was begging and praying for this not to be real so that I could just wake up soon. After the authorities talked to us, which may have been a good hour, it dawned on me that there was something I had to do. I took out my iPhone and dialed Anton's mum, crying uncontrollably as I spoke. She told me that the police had already been there and told her the devastating news. Word had traveled so quickly that within hours, the Australian consulate had contacted the Australian police and sent them to the Cavka home.

That was the hardest phone call I've ever had to make. It was now somehow about seven in the evening. Wait, how was that even possible? I could see the sun falling outside, the people on the street going about their lives like nothing had happened.

The police said something to the hotel staff, and they brought in some food and water to the conference room for us. I felt almost guilty for drinking and eating.

Anton

There was still more official business to take care of, because the police requested that we go down to the morgue to identify Anton's body that night. The morgue was something out of a movie, a concrete bunker in the middle of the jungle with open doors and windows, a bare fluorescent light fixture with insects swirling around it, shining too harshly on the metal gurneys inside. Norm and I did what we came to do, but were stuck there an extra half hour, waiting for our car ride when a monsoon rainstorm blew in.

Back at the hotel, well into the early hours of the morning, the exhaustion and adrenalin dump fully hit us. But there would be no sleep. The next day, Marjorie and Nick (Anton's mum and younger brother) would already be on a plane to Cambodia. Anton's old school friend, Jason, who lived in Thailand, also happened to be in Cambodia at that time. Jason had planned to show up to the hotel and surprise Anton.

I waited to meet Jason in the foyer of the hotel. There, I had to break the news to him that our great mate had just died the night before. I'm sure he saw it on my face before I said any words, and the pain we both felt was indescribable. Jason was a very good friend of Anton's and had even come to the very first screening of the *100-Man Fight* movie in Thailand to show his support. We both agreed that we had to keep strong and take good care of Anton's beautiful mum when she arrived, because consoling and protecting their family was the priority now.

When Marjorie and Nick arrived at Phnom Penh airport,

Jason and I were there waiting at the gate to greet them, hugging them and trying to offer some solace as best we could. It was the saddest and hardest 24 hours of my life. Marjorie decided not to take Anton's body back to Australia, but to have him cremated there at a Buddhist temple. I thought that was a great and fitting decision. The Cambodian health system doesn't regularly perform autopsies, so we still didn't know why he passed away.

That didn't stop the Cambodian media or snake-pit Facebook chat forums from speculating that Anton died of a drug overdose, which was relatively common among foreigners in gritty Phnom Penh. Of course, that couldn't have been further than the truth and Anton only had a few beers the night before. Norm contacted the media and tried responding to the forums, telling them to pull their story off the net, but I told him to stop at a certain point - it was pointless and would only fan the flames.

The official report the Australian Consulate eventually gave Marjorie stated that Anton passed away from a heart attack in his sleep. That brings some comfort. He was lying peacefully on his stomach when we found him as if he slipped away in his sleep. I later found out that Anton was messaging with our friend Scott Powell on the computer in his last hours or even minutes, chatting about how well the book was going and mentioning that he was looking forward to catching up with him later that year. According to Scott, that's when Anton just stopped responding. Scott thought he'd just fallen asleep, so I hope Anton's passing was peaceful.

Anton

Anton was not religious at all, but as spiritual and caring a person as you will find. I know that he wouldn't want people to make a fuss over him, but instead to celebrate his life over a bunch of beers, remembering him warmly. He'd encourage us to get on with our lives and say with his famous smile, "I'll be waiting for you on the other side, mate."

Two days later, Anton was cremated at a Buddhist temple surrounded by gardens, after a beautiful ceremony where monks chanted prayers and burned incense. Nick, Marjorie, Jason, Norm and I sat there solemnly, wearing what few nice clothes we'd brought along with us, paying our respects to our beautiful friend, Anton Cavka.

Words cannot explain the sorrow and heartbreak we were feeling. I cried so much; I couldn't cry anymore. My thoughts kept going to poor Marjorie, Anton's dad, Nick and Michael, Anton's other brother. My heart wept for them. There was nothing I could do but feel their pain and heartache. It all felt cloudy, like it wasn't real, but the day came when I was set to fly out of Cambodia and back to Thailand.

I was waiting in the foyer of the hotel, saying goodbye to Marjorie and Nick, who had their bags packed and ready to head off to the airport, too. We were all waiting for the funeral service coordinator to turn up with Anton's ashes.

When he got there, the funeral director handed Marjorie her son's ashes in a small box and wished her and Nick the best. He was an absolute gentleman the whole time and made Marjorie and Nick feel at ease under these devastating circumstances. I can't thank him enough for that. My taxi pulled up and it was time for me to say goodbye, so I hugged Nick and then Marjorie.

"Leaving humanity goodbye," Marjorie said.

"Pardon?" I said.

"Leaving humanity goodbye – it's written on your t-shirt," she replied.

My heart dropped. I realized that Anton had given me this t-shirt as a present.

"What? Really?!" A hot flush came over my body, reddening my face. Why did I have to wear this particular t-shirt on this day?

I hadn't even paid notice to what was written on the shirt and the font was barely readable. It was my last clean one, so I had just thrown it on. Almost ashamed to look Marjorie in the eyes, I realized the significance of those words that particular morning. Of course, I never would have worn such a t-shirt out of respect for Marjorie and Nick if I'd noticed it.

Always classy and composed, Marjorie didn't press the issue, nor did she hold any ill will. But I made my way to the taxi feeling absolutely shattered. Maybe it was the pain and guilt of this happening to Anton while we were together all hitting me at once?

As we wound our way through the bustling Phnom Penh streets towards the airport, I could only think how devastating

Anton

and traumatic it was going to be for Marjorie and Nick to have to physically carry Anton's ashes back to Australia with them.

It was such a small thing but somehow, this all became real for me when Marjorie noticed the words on my t-shirt. I held back tears as the taxi pulled up in front of the Thai Airlines entrance, putting on my sunglasses as I went inside.

CHAPTER 29: LESS THAN ZERO

浪人

Arriving back in Suvarnabhumi Airport in Bangkok, Thailand, I quickly jumped in a taxi and headed back home – about a 90-minute drive. I was actually a mess in Cambodia, completely breaking down emotionally, but I just barely managed to keep it together to give support to Marjorie and Nick.

When I got back to our house in Chonburi, I rushed inside to see my son and Mo. The moment I saw them, I broke down, sobbing, hugging them both tightly, not wanting to ever let go. Mo was crying as well and little Max just gripped on to the both of us, not understanding what was going on. Mo had fallen sick because of the news of Anton. She adored Anton and was absolutely devastated, unable to comfort me until that moment because I was so far away.

The next day, Mo was even more unwell. She had an alarmingly high fever and was so weak she could barely walk. I took her to the emergency room and the nurses quickly rushed her off when they saw the condition she was in.

I sat there in the waiting room, with my son on my lap, powerless. A dreamlike state blanketed me, and I couldn't comprehend what was happening. Would I lose my best friend and then my wife, too, in the same week? It was too much to even think about. A doctor came out about an hour later and said that Mo had to stay overnight and possibly for a few days, but that she would be okay. I almost broke down again, but this time out of relief. He said that she had the flu and was very dehydrated and so they were giving her fluids and letting her rest while they monitored her.

As I left the hospital and drove back home, my eyes filled up with tears, but I had to focus since I had Max in the car. Thank God we got back home safely. I cooked up some food for him, put the TV on and pressed play on the DVD player. It was kung fu Panda, our favorite father-and-son movie.

Somehow, the movie didn't start from the beginning, but rather started from the scene where kung fu Panda's master just died and his body is slowly dispersing, vanishing into the clouds. Before he fades away, the master's last words to his student are, "You must believe." And then he was gone.

For some strange reason, that gave me some comfort and peace.

Silly to feel better from a cartoon movie, I know. But I held onto Max and was absorbed by the moment. It had been only five days since Anton had passed away. I do believe he reached out to me then – and since, and this was one of these moments that I'll never forget.

Max and I picked up Mo from the hospital two days later. She had fully recovered, and we went back home. I would like to say that I was coping well, but the truth is that I wasn't. Just out of nowhere I would break down crying. I couldn't control it, and that scared me.

One time that week, we were at a supermarket and I was next in line at the register. The lady behind the cash register looked right through me to the person in line behind me, ready to serve them next. It was like she couldn't see me standing there, like I didn't even exist; a ghost.

That shook me up. Finally, she realized that I was next and started ringing up my groceries – an innocent mistake. But I was rattled. I told Mo that the lady couldn't see me because I should be dead. Anton should be alive, and it should have been me who died. Mo just looked at me, baffled and confused by what I was saying.

For me it made perfect sense: I was convinced that I should be dead instead of Anton. Somehow, I had cheated the reach of the Grim Reaper, but death was lurking around me, looking to correct the mistake with its eyes set on me. It had grabbed my friend and now it was coming for me.

I was slowly losing my mind. I was scared to sleep at night because I thought I would never wake up and never see my son again. Life felt that fragile. To close my eyes and sleep would be a huge risk that I would disappear, too.

Of course, this was PTSD, extreme shock and grief manifesting itself, but we don't realize that in the moment. I hadn't exactly been trained all those decades to be in touch with my feelings and mental health. I would only learn years later, not until we sat down to finish the book, that Norm experienced the same after Anton died, and was so scared of closing his eyes and sleeping because he might not wake up, too. Norm stayed in Cambodia, alone to deal with his own surreal emptiness the morning the rest of us left the hotel to go back to Aus. He actually lived in Phnom Penh for two more years, deeply affected by Anton's death for a long time.

A few weeks later and things weren't getting any better for me. Just to get an hour or two of sweaty, stirring rest at night, I had to numb my brain with a dozen beers. During the day I was agitated and depressed, with a hangover and very negative with those around me. If I ran out of beers, I would jump in the car drunk and hammer it to the bottle shop. It was like I was daring the Reaper to come and get me. I did not care. You took my best mate, so now come for me, as it should be. That would just speed up the inevitable and stop the torment. I was out of control, spiraling down very fast. My thoughts were unfamiliar to me like someone else was thinking them, my actions completely out of character.

Lying around the house all day, not training at all and just sitting there torturing myself with my thoughts, I would analyze and dissect what had happened in Cambodia, looping the details and timeline in my head. *Why did Anton have to die and not me? Why did Anton have to die and not me? Why did Anton have to die and not me?* Maybe this was what it was like to go insane, it occurred to me.

One day, my mum called me up. She was very worried. "Come home, Judd. Come home for Christmas, we miss you," she said. I didn't want to, but I needed a change and couldn't let myself drop any further – there was nowhere else to fall.

It has been five weeks since Anton passed away when the Christmas holiday approached. I tried putting on a brave face, but I was still so sad and depressed. I had no more tears left. They had dried up and all was left with an empty hole in my heart. I remember my mum saying you can never recover from the loss of someone dear to you, you just learn how to deal with it better and take it one day at a time.

I have to say this helped me a lot. I understood that my feelings were normal, and I wasn't waiting for them to suddenly go away one day anymore. That sense of control helped me a lot. It was up to me to deal with the feelings and keep living. I only had to look at Mo and Max to remember what I had to live for. My mum is the rock in the family and I can't thank her and Peter enough for being there for us.

I also have some dear friends in Australia and I'm very grateful for all of their support during those dark days. One day early on when we returned, Nick Cavka handed me a USB stick with all of the chapters that Anton and I had been working on in Cambodia. I didn't look at it for a long time. I didn't have the heart. But now, I had the courage to pop it in my computer and open it up.

Wow, it was amazing.

My heart melted with happiness, sadness and all kinds of emotions. I could hear Anton's voice as I read the chapters, almost seeing the warm glow of his face across the table from me as we worked on the book. That lifted my spirits tremendously.

Before we left Cambodia, Norm had said to me, "Let's finish this book. It will be a way to honor Anton...I am here for you, Judd."

So, I called up Norm on Skype one day early in 2016. For some reason, we hadn't talked a lot. Maybe we were both going through such a dark time and didn't feel like we wanted to bother the other, when some kinship is exactly what would have helped us both.

"Norm, if you have any time, I would love to work on the book.," I said.

He never even paused, "Let's do it. I'm ready, Judd."

So that's what we did, and the result is what you're holding in your hands and reading right now, as well as my first book, *The Young Lions*.

Finishing Anton's writing has helped me so much. It's completely changed my thought process about life, death, and what really matters with the precious time we all do have. It's brought me from being in a dark hole of depression to wanting to conquer the world again. I wanted to make Anton proud, and I know he would have wanted me to live my life to the fullest above all else.

I hope I've done that, and I hope he's smiling down at us.

CHAPTER 30:
A WHIRLWIND TOUR

浪人

Returning back to Thailand, I was filled with ambition and enthusiasm to succeed again. I poured all of my emotions and focus into launching my dream of hosting my own camps that offered the *uchi deshi* experience I had in Japan. It took a lot of planning and organization, but my first two *uchi deshi* camps went magnificently. It was incredibly fulfilling to see the young *uchi deshi* sweating and fighting and living together, but this time there in paradise-like Thailand.

Shortly after the second camp, I traveled to Hungary to support my *uchi deshi* brother, Sandor, who was putting on a world tournament. Located in his beautiful hometown of Szentes, it was great to reunite with my old *uchi deshi* brother, who I hadn't seen since 1991.

I couldn't have been more impressed with what I saw there. Shihan Sandor had his own *Kyokushin* organization, and his international tournament attracted fighters from all over the globe. He even had a memorial to honor Sosai built just for the occasion, carved out of solid rock and standing ten feet high.

That really touched my heart and I thought it showed heaps of class for him to make this beautiful monument to our teacher. Large banners of Sosai's image were also hanging on the walls of the stadium, with a huge taiko drum at the front of the stage where the fighters would walk in, just like we had at the *Honbu* dojo so many years before.

The tournament was so special because of Sandor's great efforts. He left no detail unattended and made it a prestigious event for everyone to remember. It also left a huge impression on me on how to run such an amazing tournament. I was taking mental notes the whole time, thinking that it would be great to try to emulate Sandor's hospitality and plan my own tournaments in the future. Not only did Sandor welcome me with open arms, but he arranged for me to take a seminar the day after the tournament concluded. He said, "Brother, I want you to teach the class and give them a taste of what it was like to train at *Honbu!*"

"Osu!" I answered back, as that was all I needed to say.

The seminar went really well. I pushed them hard with basics and expressed the importance of *kiai* and maintaining the attitude of giving 100 percent effort with every single punch, kick, or technique. As Sandor understood, I was only passing on what Sosai had instilled in us all those years before.

"Sweat is the only secret! *Osu!*" I yelled to the class as I wiped the sweat pouring off my brow and puddling around me.

A Whirlwind Tour

"Work the basics hard. Do not become satisfied with your training but instead strive to always improve yourself, physically, mentally, and most importantly, spiritually," I told all of these eager and dedicated students. I explained to them that in this day and age, people are always running around at a thousand miles an hour. We're glued to our phones and social media, working more than ever, and always thinking about what we have to do next.

But karate training allows you to put that all aside for an hour or two at a time, transporting you to a different world; dare I say a better time when we didn't have all of those stressors and distractions. That's why it's so important we never forget these traditions but do our best to honor them and pass them on. Even tying your belt and bowing in at the start of class should not be rushed or disregarded, as they are important rituals.

When you tie your belt, it signifies that you are ready to learn and give 100 percent. I tell the students, "My belt might be black in color, but in my mind, it's still a white belt because I'm forever a student and always learning."

Bowing in at the start of class allows us to forget about the outside world. Checking your phone, your bills, how tired you feel after a long day and all of life's frustrations, are all left at the door. It's important to train with a clear mind. That's the foundation so you can then give it your best effort and sweat it out. If you go into each day's training with the right mindset and honor these traditions, you'll leave exhausted, barely able to lift your feet as you walk out into the world once again, but you will also be elated on a spiritual and physical high.

This is the *Kyokushin* way. After attending Sandor's incredible seminar in Hungary, it really confirmed for me that my calling in life was to continue sharing Mas Oyama's ways and teachings.

Returning back to Thailand, I made it my mission to complete *The Young Lions* book. To continue the tradition and process that I'd had with Anton, I even visited Norm in the Philippines to work on the book for a few weeks. We traveled to the island of Boracay, which is often voted the #1 island in the world with its baby-powder soft sand and crystal blue waters. There, we settled into the same routine, with training on the beach in the morning and working on the book over coffee all day. Anton did such an amazing job getting it all started, and now it is time to put all the pieces together and get the book published.

Norm and I worked on the book relentlessly for about two months, long after I departed the island paradise of Boracay in the Philippines. At least once a day, we corresponded by emails as we both wrote, and often jumped on a Skype session to discuss the more difficult parts. Finally, after an excruciating editing and publishing process, the first run of books was printed in July of 2016.

I can't tell you how proud I was to finally have this book in my hands, to feel the weight, flip through the pages, and see a glimmer off the shiny black and red cover. I can't tell you how thankful I am to Norm for his support and friendship, and

A Whirlwind Tour

without him there's no way the book would have turned out as well as it did.

The Young Lions is dedicated to the memory of my great friend, Anton Cavka, and there's not a day that goes by that I don't think about my fallen brother. Anton's positive attitude and unparalleled zest for life rubbed off on me and is still invigorating me to this day.

I did everything to the best of my ability to promote the story, always thinking of how Anton would have done it, knowing full well that he would have poured his heart and soul into it if he was still around. It was finished, but I still needed to make him proud.

Anton once told me that this book was going to bring me a spotlight and allow me to travel the world doing seminars and running camps, and he was right. Once the book was released, I was even more in demand to teach and participate in camps and seminars. For three years, I traveled all around the world, doing just that as I also promoted *The Young Lions*.

The experience was amazing. Every country was special in its own way: America, France, Belgium, England, Wales, Greece, Singapore, Sweden, India, Hungary, Indonesia, and even Costa Rica. Some of these countries I visited more than once, and I also taught seminars all around Australia during this time.

I am full of gratitude for the opportunity to travel around the world and meet extraordinary, wonderful, spirited people. The world feels like a familiar, welcoming place when you've visited so many different cultures and met so many people. Without exception, everyone I met in each country was very respectful, kind and good hearted. Indeed, this is the true spirit of martial arts.

I've got so many wonderful memories from these seminars. From the early hours of morning training in the freezing Atlantic Ocean of Massachusetts; running in the big, beautiful park in Banglamore, India; beach training at Coney Island as the sun came up yelling *"fighto,"* sparring with students in the waves of Venice Beach, California as the sun went down.

I visited New York, Seattle, Boston, and even got to do a seminar with the legendary Dolph Lundgren in Los Angeles. Having lunch with Dolph, Yamaki Kenji, and Tom Callahan was something I will never forget. Of course, most people probably know Dolph Lundgren as the steely, menacing Soviet fighter Ivan Drago from the *Rocky IV* movie, but Dolph is the real deal. Before he became a movie star, he was a full-contact karate fighter. Dolph won the British Open, Australian Nationals and even competed in the 2nd World Tournament at only 20-years-old, losing to the eventual champion, Nakamura Makoto – The Bull.

Their fight is on YouTube and you can see just how incredibly strong he is. It was an absolute war. Sosai himself stepped in, insisting the fight go an extra round after a bad decision by the judge ended it prematurely. Sosai was a fan of Dolph and had the towering Swede regularly do demonstrations at his tournaments. I believe Dolph could have been world champion if he continued

A Whirlwind Tour

on with his full-contact karate career, but if he did that, the world wouldn't have Ivan Drago, who was the perfect villain for that movie. Since then, Dolph has starred in 70 more films, almost all of them action movies!

He told us a great story over lunch. While making the movie, *The Punisher* (awesome action flick!), Yamaki Kenji was playing one of the bad guys in the movie. In the script, Yamiki's character eventually dies in battle, but Dolph told us that Yamaki was not happy about that. He told the director that his parents would see the movie and get distressed if he died. We had a good laugh over that. Yamaki is a world champion and has completed the 100-man *Kumite* as well – he's tough as nails but was worried his character dying in the movie would upset his family! Funny stuff.

It was an honor to train with Dolph. His power and technique are absolutely amazing and he's also very friendly and down to earth; he embodies the best of what *Kyokushin* is all about in my eyes.

In my travels, I also got to witness the 3000-year-old Acropolis in Athens, leaving me speechless and in awe. I saw the venerable and solemn castles of Wales; took in Antwerp's train station that was built during the Napoleon era; and enjoyed the quaint country town of Lille in France, which looked like something out of a movie.

But one of the biggest highlights of my trips was also visiting the old apartment in Earls Court, London where we used to live when I was a child. I was able to reunite with my old primary school principal, giving her a copy of *The Young Lions*, and telling her how thankful I was to be able to attend her school as a young kid. I bet she never thought I'd write and publish a book!

My Aussie camps and seminars allowed me to travel from one side of this great continent to the other: Port Macquarie, Parkes, Sydney, Canberra, Griffith, Perth, Queensland, and the great Ocean Road at Anglesea Beach, one of the most beautiful beaches in the world. Training there made it all the more special, and the camps and travel just flew by like in a blur. It was a roller coaster ride, but I was living every martial artist's dream and loving every moment of it.

CHAPTER 31: UCHI DESHI CAMP/FIGHTO

浪人

In early March of 2016, my dream of running my own *uchi deshi* camp was realized, all thanks to Dean and Anton's vision and encouragement. The aim was to bring *karateka* from all over the world to Thailand for six of the most intensive and challenging days of their lives, living, eating, and training together like we did at the *Honbu* dojo.

The first camp was actually twelve days, which proved to be too long based on the intensity of the training and difficulty for most people to get off work and travel to Thailand for two whole weeks instead of one.

Five years later, I'm proud to say that the Judd Reid *uchi deshi* Fight Camp is still running strong, with more than 100 people having taken part. Marital arts students from all around the world attend these camps. Some of them are people I know well and have trained with before, or students at dojos in Australia. Others have attended my seminars in some other country. There are even people who just message me online and inquire about the camp, complete strangers who have the intestinal fortitude to show up and thrust themselves into something completely unknown.

I give all of the camp's attendees credit because no matter where they're coming from, they have to make the long journey to Thailand. Not only are they tired from traveling, but they have to adjust to a new time change, which is most difficult for those coming from Europe or the U.S., where literally night is day. Everyone also needs to adjust to the new food, and extremes in heat and humidity.

With all of that, we train three times a day and really give it our all, so just making it through the week is a massive accomplishment.

The camp is set in Jomtien, which is a beautiful, serene seaside town only about an hour and a half from Bangkok. It's just far enough from the hustle and bustle of nearby Pattaya (the Thai version of Las Vegas), but just close enough that it's easy and convenient.

I hold the camp at a resort on sprawling grounds filled with perfectly manicured lawns, gardens, and swimming pools. The somewhat secluded resort sits on a cliff overlooking the sea. There is a nice stone staircase (more on that later!) leading down to our own private beach where we do a lot of training.

For those who have never been to Thailand, it's a very safe and organized place to travel, and Thai culture is so friendly and inviting. It's the perfect place to visit for a week and train the hardest they've ever trained. Within those carefully orchestrated six days, I want to give them the same sort of experience I had in Japan under Sosai Mas Oyama. I don't go as far as to deny them air conditioning and have them sleep on the floor on bamboo matts, but they do all share rooms, which really boosts comradery, and we all eat meals together.

I even gave them a taste of my traditional breakfast that I had in Japan, a mixture of rice, miso soup, nori (seaweed), raw egg, and natto (fermented beans). We had this every single day in Japan, and it offers fantastic protein and nutrition, although the smell is more than a little unnerving.

Serving it at the Thailand camp one morning (I don't make them eat it every day!) was a great way to give them an authentic experience from my 1,000 days of live-in training. Plus, if I'm honest, it's always fun to see their faces and reactions as they eat it. Of course, they all finish it – eventually – as they don't have a choice!

But the Thailand camp is really about training hard, and we take that seriously. Each day starts with a 6 a.m. session. So, the *uchi deshi* start to congregate at our meeting place outside as early as 5:30 a.m. to stretch, loosen up, and wake up a little in the pre-dawn darkness.

Sometimes I will take the group on a slow run on the beach. It's still dark at this time, so I make everyone keep close together, trusting the person in front of them not to stumble. By day three, everyone is thoroughly sore, so these early morning sessions running on the beach are important for the *uchi deshi* to gain energy by working as a group.

"Fighto! Fighto!" I yell in cadence as we run. "Fighto" is the rallying cry that means to keep fighting, to persevere, and to endure. The word echoes off the beach and over the water as the *uchi deshi* run up and back, up and back, sand and ocean splashing them. This lifts their spirits and it's what they need when they feel they can't not go on. The morning sessions are all about conditioning and fitness. I make sure we train outside of our comfort zones, soaking wet with feet dragging along the sand.

A few times each week, I ran the group up the long, ascending road from our hotel, and then another couple of kilometers to a park that sits on a sheer hill. There, a strip of pavement winds precipitously at a more than 45-degree angle, known as the Buddha Hill or Hill of Death. Yes, it's the same hill I sprinted up thousands of times in preparation for my 100- man *Kumite* many years ago!

The whole group lines up at the bottom and GO! The sprint is on, which is 20 seconds of pure hell for your cardio. Then, we walk down just enough to catch our breath and do it again. And again. And again. Of course, I watch the group for injuries, but I do want to push them well past the point of exhaustion, and the fighters are often dizzy or even sometimes throw up. If nothing else, the Buddha Hill will keep you honest, and it's become a dreaded (and loved) rite of passage for my *uchi deshi* camps.

During these morning sessions, nothing is pretty – it's straight brutal conditioning. We don't train in fancy sports clothes, but all black *uchi deshi* shorts and matching tee-shirts. We don't have music or headphones, only our inner voices screaming to keep going. Fighto!

In the mornings, we always mix it up with push-ups on our knuckles, sit-ups, body weight exercises, and plenty of body conditioning by punching and kicking each other, all soaking wet in sweat and sea water, covered in sand. After the morning session it was still only 7:30 a.m. or so, and we felt like we really started the day right. We all met for a big healthy breakfast a half hour later and it was well earned.

Our next session starts at 10:30 a.m. promptly in the hotel's ballroom, which they graciously allowed us to convert into a dojo. The carpeted floors are lined with matts and I have posters and banners related to Kyokushin adorning the walls, including paying homage to Sosai Oyama, who oversees it all. We always wear our dogis in these mid-morning sessions and end with the *dojo Kun* (oath). I also stress that they should learn Japanese etiquette as well as terminology, paying respect to the martial way.

In this session, we cover a lot of techniques and combinations, focusing on footwork and drilling until we get everything precise. Sometimes, I'll hold these mid-morning sessions on the spacious, perfect green lawn outside. Dealing with the heat is an extra challenge but the view always makes it worth it

At my Thailand *uchi deshi* fight camps, the third and last training of the day was at 3:30 pm. These sunset sessions, as I like to call them, are really special – and some of the hardest. We'd start in the hotel's dojo in clean dogis, everyone ready to give it their all despite the aches, pains, soreness, and fatigue.

Remember that we do at least 18 highly intense hour-and-a-half workouts in only six days. For most people training at home at their dojo, they maybe make it there to train a couple times a week, or two to three hours of training. So, during the camp, they might get three months' worth of training in just one week.

The body doesn't have time to recover properly, and so it enters survival mode. Sleep is what you need most for your body to recover, but it's often hard for the camp's fighters to sleep well. They toss and turn due to pain and injuries, adrenaline coursing through their bodies that they can't switch off, and the time change doesn't help of course. Some people sleep great, but others only get a few hours per night.

The injuries definitely mount up, too. Everyone has aches and pains, and there are a lot of knuckles with no skin, battered and swollen shins, feet, knees, and ankles, and bruises all over. I make it a point that we spar every day and there is a lot of body conditioning, so they get the full fighter experience – and remember what *Kyokushin* is all about: training to fight, not just to train.

Over the course of years of camps and hundred-or-so

participants, we've had plenty of dislocations, a few blown-out knees, and more than a few broken ribs. Most of the time, these fighters choose to keep going. Of course, I tell them to work around their injuries and do what they can. The goal is never to get seriously hurt, but I always applaud their true fighting spirit when they choose to march on despite being injured.

Like I always tell them, "The times when your body is fatigued, and you don't feel like training are often the best times for training. It's funny how the human body works. These times end up being some of your best training sessions."

At the end of a long day, the best relief is visiting one of the professional massage salons on the road by our resort, where they do an amazing job massaging our feet and legs to release the lactic acid and loosen everything up. It makes a big difference! There's a whole row of massage spas, authentic Thai restaurants, great cafes, barber shops, 7-11s, and our laundry place on the strip. Driving or walking by, you'll see dozens of *dogis* hanging outside to dry, and the hotel also gives us access to the second-floor roof deck to dry all of our *dogis* and training gear.

But the whole point of the training is to bring them to their limit and then watch them smash right past it. Everyone gets broken down by the training and lack of recovery time, but, by day three or four, they stop listening to their minds screaming "stop!" and just go for it anyways, tapping into something primal. And our chants of "Fighto!" and a loud "Osu!" when training always helps muster energy and fighting spirit.

I'm always amazed at everyone's progress from the beginning of the camp to the end. Even though these fighters come into the camp in good shape and have been training at home regularly, they are huffing and puffing the first day or two. But by the end, they can do punching and kicking drills for half an hour straight, with burpees in between and no rest, like machines!

Each fighter is good at something and needs improvement at other aspects of their training. Some are great runners and tremendous athletes and breeze through the conditioning. Some are very comfortable with the sparring, while others don't have as much fighting experience. And others have mastered the *Kata*, know the terms, and dojo *Kun* in Japanese, or are very familiar with the techniques. But everyone has their challenges and shortcomings that they have to face head-on, and that's part of the process of growing as a fighter and *Kyokushin* practitioner.

So, for our sunset sessions, we start in the dojo and do some regular warm-ups and drills, but anticipation of the sparring ahead has everyone on razor's edge. At some point, I have everyone form two lines facing each other, and the sparring begins, "Hajime!" I have them spar each other for about 90-second rounds, then stop, bow, move one person down the line, and the sparring starts again immediately.

We punch each other with bare knuckles as hard as we can (except in the face or head), and kick anywhere, including the head. I do have the camp's fighters wear thin padded shin guards but there are no gloves or even hand wraps – strengthening your fists until they are like rocks is important. There are also knees and elbows to the chest, similar to Muay Thai.

During these late afternoon sparring sessions, everyone really gives it their all and shows tremendous courage and effort. I encourage them to use the techniques and combinations we've learned, and impress upon them that in *Kyokushin*, we never want to take a step back or give any ground. If your enemy is overtaking you, switch stances or move at an angle. Or even better, go even harder forward at them – but never move straight back, which shows weakness. I always share what Sosai Oyama always told us, which is that our opponent feels fear and pain, too. They are just men and not Gods, so never stop and keep pushing forward.

Once everyone has sparred with each other, I might keep going for round two or three, but usually have everyone take off their shin guards, grab their water bottle, and we walk outside, down the stone staircase to the beach. There, as the sun is just starting to fall towards the horizon over the ocean, we start a jog up and down the beach, staying in formation and chanting "Fight-o!" with commitment and pride as we go. Unlike the morning training sessions on the beach which are in our fight camp shorts and t-shirts, we're now still wearing our *dogis*. When they get soaking wet with sea water and covered in sand it adds about 3 kilos, so it's like training with a weighted vest.

After a lot of sparring and more running on the beach, it's time for more conditioning. We do push-ups on our knuckles on the flagstone floor or on the sand, carry each other up the stone stairs piggy-back, do handstand push-ups or wheelbarrows with a partner on our knuckles, and plenty of frog squats up the stone staircase. Always squats!

Next, I'll lead them in some *Kata* facing the ocean as the sun goes down. And finally, we usually do more sparring or body conditioning drills while standing up to our waists in the ocean.

Hot, fatigued, and bashed up – but never defeated – it's a relief for everyone to dive into the waves and splash around after our training concludes. Dean and I always jump right in with them. In one of my first camps, that lead to a funny situation that I've never told anyone about, but I'll tell you now.

After our afternoon session we all slog up the stone stairs and into the hotel and up to our rooms, still dripping wet. Well, one time I got back to my room and took off my *dogi* while in the shower to wash off the sea water and sand. To my shock, a small fish popped out of my *dogi* and fell on the shower floor! Of course, he must have gotten caught there in the ocean and smuggled a ride, but I never even realized it was in there!

Jumping in the ocean immediately after our sunset sessions is one of the most fun times for everyone. But for me, it's also one of the most fulfilling, watching the happiness on their faces, splashing around in paradise after the hardest training day they've ever had, knowing they'd earned it. As the sessions and days go on, I can see newfound strength and confidence in each of them, as well as comradery. There have been plenty of genuine friendships formed at this camp between people from all over the world who sometimes don't even share a first language, other than the strong common bond of having trained and survived together.

So far, there have been more than 20 different countries represented at the camps, from South America to the U.S. and Canada, plenty of European nations, Asia, Australia, and New Zealand, of course. We've had an Iranian woman, Mahdiyeh, who did a great job, which I think is truly amazing – a testament to how *Kyokushin* can bring us all together, as Sosai Oyama used to say.

Our camp is open to everyone of all ages, genders, religions, and skill levels. I've had people who have a wrestling or boxing background join. And it's completely non-political, as *Kyokushin* training should be. As long as you come with fire in your belly to give it your best, that's all that matters to me, so everyone is welcome.

I've had kids as young as 11-year-old Kyan Redfern at the camps, and as old as 68-year-old Tom Foxlee. Sébastien and Celine from Belgium, Darren Jordan Shihan, Russ, and Lirim Sulaj, Alicia and Tiani Smith, Vinayak Shetty, Tyson Lawes, Mitch Cook, Rinny Jr. from India, Joe Wells from Australia, and my writer buddy, Norm Schriever, have all attended three camps. In fact, Norm had never done karate before when he joined my very first camp. He broke three ribs in the first few days of the 12-day session but decided to keep going, finishing strong.

Of course, I couldn't have done these camps without the help of one of my best mates, Dean Booth. Dean deserves all of the credit and thanks because, after all, it was his idea to start these camps! He is indispensable in helping me plan, organize, and run the camps and all the training.

And he sure helps me learn everyone's name, which can be challenging for us when there are 25 new fighters showing up on the first day. But by the end of the week, we all know each other well and have really pushed ourselves like champions.

In the very last session of the camp, we do a lot of hard sparring, and there are usually a few grading tests with full *Kumite* and testing. Finally, I may award a new belt to those fighters, and we conclude with photos, a lot of hugging, pats on the back, and congratulations. Each *uchi deshi* is awarded a certificate for their outstanding effort and achievement.

But the closing festivities are just the beginning, as everyone showers, dresses up a little, and comes back downstairs to meet in the hotel lobby. We all walk next door to an adjacent resort, which is really an unforgettable place with a fascinating backstory. But that's a secret only reserved for those who finish the camp!

As a big, happy, exhausted group, we all sit out on the deck overlooking the Thai sea at sundown, ordering heaps of local dishes, eating and drinking to our heart's content, just like Sosai would do at our Saturday night special dinners.

After that, camp is done. They have officially completed the Judd Reid *Uchi Deshi* Thailand Fight Camp, a source of confidence and badge of honor for the rest of their lives. Some fighters leave

Uchi Deshi Camp/Fighto

in a day or two, while some stay around for a vacation in Thailand and a chance to let their bumps and bruises heal up. Most people have to jump on a plane and get back home and back to work quickly. Can you imagine being back at work at your desk the Monday morning after that experience?! I give them all the credit in the world for making that long journey and giving it their all like true soldiers.

CHAPTER 32: CHIKARA

浪人

In March of 2018, shortly after the fifth *uchi deshi* camp in Thailand, Mo, Max and I returned to Australia to start the next chapter in our lives.

At that time, Max was four years old and due to start primary school, so that was one big factor why we decided to come back to my home country. Thailand is such a beautiful nation and an easy place to live, but we thought it was best to give Max an Australian upbringing and schooling. To be honest, I also missed my family and friends dearly.

For years, we'd gone back and forth between Thailand and Australia, but now it was time to settle more permanently. Once we returned to Melbourne, we moved in with my parents and I immediately went back to teaching at the Chikara Dojo once again.

Josh Cooke and Shoba Hariharan took over and did a magnificent job running the dojo while I was away. I'm thankful for their great work. It was so nice to see all the students and families again, who had been loyal and supported the dojo for many years. Aside from teaching again at Chikara dojo, the Essendon Football Team heard I was back and called to see if I wanted my old job back as a boxing, strength and conditioning trainer. Of course, I said yes!

I also returned back to training at the SHOP (Soldiers House of Pain) with Ned and the boys. We'd started these SHOP Tuesday night sessions 25 years ago, and Ned, Costa, and the boys pretty much hadn't missed a day. A few new guys had joined our Tuesday training sessions: Chris Vlahogiannis, Aaron Goodson, Tristan Papadopoulos, Tony and Lucas Karlusic, and Chris and Callum Brett, and they all gave it their very best.

One of the original SHOP members, Michael Dugina, had been working with the Collingwood Football Team after 25 years in a role similar to mine with Essendon. That made him one of the longest-working strength and conditioning coaches in the game, and he was highly respected by his team – and their opponents.

Dugina was still writing out workout routines for us to follow for our SHOP sessions. As always, they were challenging, tortuous, and a whole lot of fun. It felt great to be back training with these awesome guys again! Within weeks back in Oz, I had pretty much returned to my routine like nothing had changed. I think Mo and Max loved it just as much, as Mo loved the coffee shops and Max couldn't get enough of the parks.

Teaching at Chikara Dojo was a great part-time job. We ran

classes three nights a week at a gymnastic center called Team Adrenalin in Footscray. Mel Presti and Stephen Santo are brother and sister, and, along with their family, they ran a wildly successful center. Their business had grown a lot in four years. Each night, they had hundreds of dedicated students training at their center. Mel and Steve are such lovely people, extremely passionate about what they do, and I'm grateful to them for letting us use their space.

After I witnessed how quickly their business had thrived, I got a spark to start my own dojo. One day, I pulled Ned aside and spoke to him about perhaps opening a full-time space myself. He was incredibly encouraging from the beginning, and even said that he would provide support and speak with some of the other guys to see if they would help, too. Pretty soon, Ned Vrselja, Steve Romic, and Joe Haddad all offered to finance my dream of opening up a dojo.

My excitement doubled every day. This was an incredible opportunity for me and my family, and the best way for me to give back to our Chikara students. I immediately started looking around for commercial properties and factories that might house the new dojo. My good mate and training partner from the old days, Russ, told me about a property available in Footscray not far from the current dojo.

We quickly organized a meeting with Ned, Steve, Joe, and Russ to check the place out. When I first saw it, I knew it would be perfect. The building was a brand-new three-story building constructed of concrete with large, double-glazed sliding glass doors in front. Its location on Hyde Street was perfect, close to the city and very near schools, public transport, parks, restaurants, and other amenities.

I instantly fell in love with the space and saw the huge potential it had. We all agreed that it was exactly what we were looking for. Thanks to my awesome mates and support team, we'd managed to find the dojo of our dreams! Russ's friend, Dean Johnson, was the owner of the building, which helped tremendously when it came to securing a lease. After only ten days, I signed the contract for a 15-year lease - there was no turning back now!

Within a few months, our permits came through, allowing us to operate as a karate school and we had the inside area fitted out. If you think finishing a 100-man *Kumite* is painful, you should try navigating the business permit process in Melbourne!

The moment our permits were approved, Highrise Carpentry, Ned and Anton Karaula's construction business, got to work. They did an incredible job outfitting the building as a dojo, surpassing even my wildest expectations. I'd especially like to thank Jack Roberts, who did a lot of the work. Jack is one of Ned and Anton's main workers. It is incredible what these carpenters can do. I have no doubt that the pyramids were built by humans now that I've witnessed what Jack and Highrise Carpentry can build! Two of the Chikara student's parents, David Caputo (Kapitol Construction) and Charlie Ridis, also helped in the building process. When it came time to start branding and marketing my vision, the incredible Todd Reeves was gracious enough to do all of my artwork. It was a real team effort and I feel so grateful – then and to this day - to have such great friends supporting me.

On February 16th, 2019, we officially opened the Chikara Dojo. It was the culmination of many months of hard work, planning, and sacrifice on the part of a whole lot of people.

If I were to walk you through the dojo, the ground floor is where we have our reception area and the strength & conditioning gym. We also have a boxing ring and ten large boxing heavy bags hanging within that 200-square-meter space.

That first-floor area can be used for all kinds of training, and we have the latest fun (and torturous) equipment, including rowing machines, skiers, bikes, and sleds to really get your heart rate skyrocketing.

The gym has more of a grungy, sweat-factory kind of feel compared to the dojo upstairs. So, I've given this gym the nickname "SHOP 2," or Soldiers House of Pain 2 after Ned's homemade gym. On our boxing, strength & conditioning nights, I always remind people that this is a SHOP workout so we must work hard and live up to that name!

Leading up to the dojo on the second floor is a staircase lined with pictures from my Thailand fight camps and the seminars I've visited over the years. I tried to model this all after the *Honbu dojo* in Japan. The concrete walls are lined with pine, adding a distinct Japanese feel, and I even built a shrine at the front of the dojo featuring Sosai's picture.

On either side of Sosai's photograph are a few mementos that mean a lot to me, like the graduation plaque that I received from Sosai, the diary I used to write in on my long train rides back home from the dojo as a teenager, my 3rd *Dan* black belt that I received from Sosai, a copy of *The Young Lions*, and a picture of Anton. On the other side of Sosai's picture is a plaque that was awarded to me for winning a tournament in Japan, made out of copper and engraved with the famous image of Sosai wrestling with a bull.

The *dojo* upstairs also has six heavy bags hanging up, as well as tree logs at the back of the *dojo* which we hit to strengthen our hands. I also have a Taiko (Japanese Drum) standing next to the shrine, which is used to signal the start and end of each class, keeping the tradition from my time in Japan.

There is a comfortable sitting area for parents, divided by glass from the dojo so there are no distractions or interruptions from onlookers, but they can see everything clearly.

With every detail of the Chikara Dojo, I tried my best to keep the design and layout very traditional, creating its own Japanese-style world for students to train hard and learn *Kyokushin* Karate the right way.

I've been very fortunate since returning to Australia. Life is good and I regularly get to catch up with my mentor and great friend, Manny Tsivoglou. Mo, Max, and all the students at Chikara adore him dearly, and we treasure every moment we can spend with him. Manny and I love to talk about the old days

Chikara

when we trained at the Elwood dojo underneath Shihan Eddie and Wada Sensei. All we cared about back then was training and getting stronger. I guess nothing much has really changed - except hopefully we're a little wiser now, too! Those days seem like a lifetime ago, but I realize now that they changed my fate forever.

I was only 15 years old, traveling two hours each way by public transport to get to the dojo. Manny San was like an older brother to me, always encouraging and supportive. Without him, I would never have gone to Japan and certainly not be where I am right now. Thank you, Manny, for always pushing me in the right direction and being a huge positive influence in my life.

Chikara dojo has been up and running for two years now. We've survived eight months of being shut down because of the global pandemic but have bounced back twice as strong. Within a couple of months of reopening, we have more students than ever. My good old friends Duncan, Josh, and Russ are helping me with the classes, and I have some young guns, Dom, Daniel, Genci, Maja, Alessandra, and Irini helping out with the junior classes.

Now that I have my own dojo, sometimes I lay wide awake at night, thinking of different ways I can make my students stronger. When students are preparing for upcoming tournaments, I worry if they are eating sufficient food and getting enough rest. Of course, I want to push them to exhaustion and beyond their limits, turning each of them into fighting machines. But along the way, my relationship with them grows, becoming more like a family.

It's a real honor to be able to teach and have this special connection with my students, sharing this wonderful journey together. I understand now a little of what Sosai felt all those years with us at the *Honbu dojo*. And Sosai's words and philosophies always stay dear to me, always ringing true. I can still hear his voice, offering his life wisdom and encouragement all the time. It makes me realize why I've devoted my life to karate. To explain it concisely, I'd turn to the words that are written on my graduation certificate, the Wakajishiryo Certificate of Completion (graduation young lion's certificate):

We hereby certify that you have been enduring the severe and demanding dormitory life of a personal student of MAS OYAMA for three years and that you have been fully devoted to our Japanese Karate.

Therefore, we expect you will be a more advanced and devoted person able to contribute to peace and good relationships throughout the world as a young lion with an indomitable Kyokushin Spirit.

I hold these words close to my heart and try my best to honor Sosai and my long-lost friend, Anton Cavka, every single day.

Osu.

AFTERWORD

浪人

With my own dojo established, my biggest dreams are now accomplished. So, it's time again to make new goals, as the journey never ends. Here at Chikara, the wheels are turning fast!

I've been fortunate to organize and host some exciting full-contact karate events. In 2019, we invited a team over from Japan to fight our local Aussie boys. Noriyuki Tanaka KWF Shihan brought his strongest fighters. By all accounts, the audience was blown away. They had never seen that caliber of fighting before. The Japanese team won convincingly, but the Aussies showed tremendous spirit and learned a lot from the experience.

I plan to host many more events. My hope with these tournaments is to showcase just how strong and spectacular *Kyokushin* karate is. I believe whole-heartedly that *Kyokushin* karate has much to offer the world, and these tournaments are an excellent way to share that message, exposing future students to the *Kyokushin* way of life.

After all, it was Sosai Mas Oyama's world tournaments

that put *Kyokushin* on the map, producing millions of students worldwide. The whole essence of *Kyokushin* is about fighting, and *Kumite* is so integral to what we do. These events are held just down the road from Chikara Dojo, and I'm forever grateful and humbled that the word is getting out there, and our numbers are growing. Our most recent 8-man eliminator tournament was very successful and well attended. Our juniors Genci, Domenic and Maja won their undercard fights and Nathan Phillips won the whole thing, and I'm super proud of all the fighters' efforts and my juniors that fought that day.

My son's school, Footscray City Primary, is just down the road, and he's my little marketing tool! But in all seriousness, I'm thrilled that Max is interested in *Kyokushin* karate, too. As a father, I try not to push him too much. I don't want to burn him out. But he's doing great, enjoying his training and making new friends at the dojo. I'm super proud of him.

We also started a new brand of training gear called Fighto, which is doing really well. Daniel Casarella and Peter Velk, two New York lads and passionate *karatekas*, are the driving force behind Fighto, and I'm excited every time I see someone wear it. The idea for the Fighto brand came to me when I did a seminar in New York three years ago. We were running on the beach at Coney Island in the early hours of the morning, shuffling our feet through the sand and yelling "fighto!" in perfect unison. It occurred to me that it would be great to have training gear that represents our unity and fighting spirit. Together with Daniel and Peter, we pushed to get Fighto merchandise out there worldwide.

Afterword

I should also mention how appreciative Mo and I are for all the support we get from the Chikara students and parents. We place a big emphasis on family here at Chikara, as we focus on building better people, not just better fighters. So, seeing the students, mums, dads, and kids training side-by-side, creating stronger bonds, puts a big smile on my face. It's an experience that's unique to martial arts and it's a great pleasure to be a part of it. My ultimate hope is that the Chikara Dojo can produce people of high character who are respectful, kind, confident, always humble, and dedicated to serving others, with the hearts of warriors. This is the martial art way.

During these troubled times with a worldwide pandemic, it's made us all reassess what's most important in life. I was so busy running the dojo, I had very little time for anything else. We were able to offer online training five nights a week, making the best of a tough situation. Our spirit and resolve were definitely tested, but I feel we all came out the better for it.

I also wanted to make the best use of my time in lockdown, and it came to me that it was high time to pick up Anton's notes and chapters and finish what he'd started before his tragic passing. So, I reached out to my good friend and brother, Norm Schriever. As always, Norm didn't even hesitate and said, "Let's do it, Judd-O!" immediately. Together we finished the book that's in your hands over the course of nearly a year.

That's also the reason why *The Ronin Years* is now complete. Norm and I finished this book in honor of Anton. There's not a day that goes by I don't think about my best friend, so finishing this project brought a lot of comfort and even closure. Now I'm absolutely certain he's looking down, proud.

I hope you enjoyed *The Ronin Years* as much as we did writing it. I sincerely appreciate everyone's time to read this book and wish you all the best.

Live life to the fullest and please always remember Sosai's words: "Yareba dekiru."

You must try, you can do it!

Osu!

-Judd Reid

Made in the USA
Columbia, SC
21 May 2021